Collins

AQA GCSE 9-1
Physics
Foundation

Practice Papers

Lynn Pharaoh

Contents

SET A

SET B

Acknowledgements

The author and publisher are grateful to the copyright holders for permission to use quoted materials and images.

Every effort has been made to trace copyright holders and obtain their permission for the use of copyright material. The author and publisher will gladly receive information enabling them to rectify any error or omission in subsequent editions. All facts are correct at time of going to press.

Published by Collins
An imprint of HarperCollinsPublishers
1 London Bridge Street
London SE1 9GF

HarperCollinsPublishers
Macken House, 39/40 Mayor Street Upper,
Dublin 1, D01 C9W8, Ireland

© HarperCollinsPublishers Limited 2019

ISBN 9780008321444

First published 2019
This edition published 2022

10 9 8 7 6 5 4

All rights reserved. No part of this publication may be reproduced, stored in a retrieval system, or transmitted, in any form or by any means, electronic, mechanical, photocopying, recording or otherwise, without the prior permission of Collins.

British Library Cataloguing in Publication Data.

A CIP record of this book is available from the British Library.

Commissioning Editor: Kerry Ferguson
Project Leaders and Management: Chantal Addy and Shelley Teasdale
Author: Lynn Pharaoh
Cover Design: Sarah Duxbury and Kevin Robbins
Inside Concept Design: Ian Wrigley
Text Design and Layout: QBS Learning
Production: Karen Nulty
Printed and bound in the UK using 100% Renewable Electricity at CPI Group (UK) Ltd

This book is produced from independently certified FSC™ paper to ensure responsible forest management.

For more information visit: www.harpercollins.co.uk/green

Collins

AQA

GCSE

PHYSICS

F

SET A – Paper 1 Foundation Tier

Author: Lynn Pharaoh

Time allowed: 1 hour 45 minutes

Materials

For this paper you must have:
• a ruler • a calculator. • the Physics Equation Sheet (found at the end of the paper).

Instructions

- Answer **all** questions in the spaces provided.
- Do all rough work in this book. Cross through any work you do not want to be marked.

Information

- There are 100 marks available on this paper.
- The marks for questions are shown in brackets.
- You are expected to use a calculator where appropriate.
- You are reminded of the need for good English and clear presentation in your answers.
- When answering questions 03.1, 08.2 and 11.4 you need to make sure that your answer:
  – is clear, logical, sensibly structured
  – fully meets the requirements of the question
  – shows that each separate point or step supports the overall answer.

Advice

- In all calculations, show clearly how you work out your answer.

Name: _____

01.1 A plastic ruler becomes **positively charged** when rubbed with a cloth.

Explain why.

....

....

.... **[2 marks]**

01.2 Name the type of charge produced on the **cloth**.

.... **[1 mark]**

01.3 The surface of a small metal ball has been given positive charge.

This is shown in **Figure 1.1**

Figure 1.1

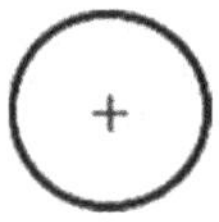

Draw **at least four** electric field lines on the diagram to show the electric field created by the charge.

[2 marks]

01.4 Describe what would happen to a tiny negatively charged particle of dust in the air near to the charged metal ball.

Explain why this would happen.

....

.... **[2 marks]**

02 Coconut oil, used in cooking, changes from a solid to a liquid when it is heated.

02.1 Describe **two** changes to the arrangement and movement of the particles when coconut oil changes from a solid to a liquid.

1. ....

....

2. ....

.... **[2 marks]**

02.2 The specific latent heat of fusion of coconut oil is 250 000 J/kg

Calculate the thermal energy needed to change 0.40 kg of coconut oil from solid to liquid.

Use the following equation.

thermal energy for a change of state = mass × specific latent heat

Give the correct unit with your answer.

....

....

Thermal energy = ...

Unit: ....

[3 marks]

Question 2 continues on the next page

02.3 A sample of coconut oil is heated at a constant rate.

The graph in **Figure 2.1** shows how the temperature of the oil changes as time passes.

Figure 2.1

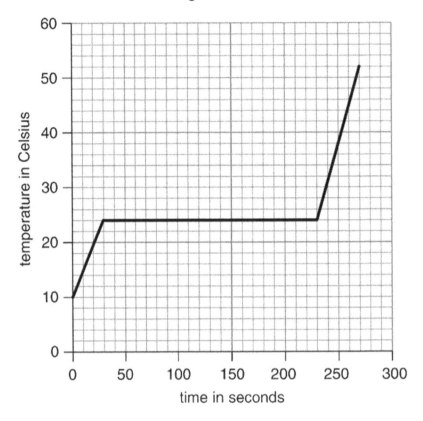

Use **Figure 2.1** to determine the melting point of coconut oil.

Melting point = ... °C

[1 mark]

02.4 Use **Figure 2.1** to determine the time taken for the coconut oil to melt completely.

....

Time taken = ... s

[1 mark]

03   A student learns that the density of a material can be found from the following equation:

$$\text{density} = \frac{\text{mass}}{\text{volume}}$$

The student is asked to determine the density of a rectangular metal block from a school laboratory materials kit.

03.1 Describe a method that the student could follow to determine the density of the block.

Include the measuring instruments that should be used.

....

....

....

....

....

....

....

....

....   **[4 marks]**

Question 3 continues on the next page

03.2 The materials kit contains three rectangular blocks, each made of a different metal.

The blocks are labelled **A**, **B** and **C**.

All three blocks have the same length, width and height.

The mass of each block is shown in **Table 3.1**

The density of the metals used in the materials kit is shown in **Table 3.2**

Table 3.1

Block	A	B	C
Mass in g	157	143	178

Table 3.2

Metal	zinc	steel	nickel
Density in g/cm³	7.1	7.8	8.9

Identify the metal in each of the three blocks.

Choose from **zinc**, **steel** and **nickel**.

A ....

B ....

C ....   **[3 marks]**

04   There are 37 known isotopes of iodine.

04.1 Explain what is meant by the term **isotope**.

....

....   **[2 marks]**

04.2 The symbol for a nucleus of one of the isotopes of iodine is:

$$^{127}_{53}I$$

Give the numbers of protons, neutrons and electrons in an atom of this isotope.

Protons: ....

Electrons: ....

Neutrons: ....   **[3 marks]**

04.3 Another isotope of iodine is iodine-131

Iodine-131 undergoes radioactive decay.

Describe what is meant by **radioactive decay**.

....

....   **[2 marks]**

04.4 Iodine-131 decays by emitting a beta particle.

Explain what is meant by **emitting a beta particle.**

....

....   **[2 marks]**

Question 4 continues on the next page

04.5 **Figure 4.1** shows the recorded count-rate from a sample of iodine-131 over 20 days.

Figure 4.1

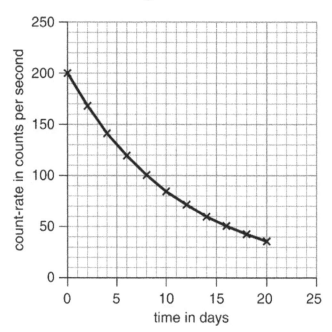

Use the graph to determine an accurate value for the half-life of iodine-131

Show how you obtain your answer.

Half-life = ... days **[3 marks]**

05.1 **Table 5.1** shows the typical power rating of some household electrical appliances.

Table 5.1

Appliance	hair dryer	laptop	iron	printer	electric kettle
Power in W	1800	60	1000	25	2000

What do the **three** highest power appliances have in common?

....

[1 mark]

05.2 Write down the equation that links energy transferred, power and time.

....

[1 mark]

05.3 An LED TV has a normal operating power rating of 50 W

Calculate the energy transferred by the TV if it is used continuously for 5 hours.

....

....

Energy transferred = ... J **[3 marks]**

05.4 The TV is used for 5 hours every day for one week.

Calculate the energy transferred by the TV in this week.

....

Energy transferred = ... J **[1 mark]**

06   A system is an object or a group of objects.

06.1 Draw a line from each system to its store of energy.

| A stretched spring |
| A football that has just been kicked |

| Elastic potential energy |
| Thermal energy |
| Chemical energy |
| Kinetic energy |

[2 marks]

06.2 A child rides her bicycle at 6.0 m/s

The mass of the child and her bicycle is 50 kg

Calculate the store of kinetic energy of the cyclist and her bicycle.

Use the following equation.

$$\text{kinetic energy} = 0.5 \times \text{mass} \times (\text{speed})^2$$

Store of kinetic energy = ... J   [2 marks]

06.3 Write down the equation that links gravitational potential energy, mass, gravitational field strength and height.

....   [1 mark]

06.4 The child now rides her bicycle to the top of a small hill and stops.

The height of the hill is 10 m

Gravitational field strength = 9.8 N/kg

Calculate the increase in the store of gravitational potential energy of the child and her bicycle.

_____

Increase in gravitational potential energy store = _____ J **[2 marks]**

06.5 The child now freewheels down the hill on her bicycle.

At the bottom of the hill she reaches a speed of 8.0 m/s

Calculate the store of kinetic energy of the child and her bicycle at the bottom of the hill.

_____

Store of kinetic energy = _____ J **[2 marks]**

06.6 Calculate the amount of energy that is dissipated as she freewheeled from the top to the bottom of the hill.

_____

Energy dissipated = _____ J **[1 mark]**

07 A metal block is heated to 100°C

The hot metal block is then put into a beaker of water at room temperature.

07.1 The temperature of the water increases by 10°C

The mass of water in the beaker is 0.10 kg

The specific heat capacity of water is 4200 J/kg °C

Calculate the **increase** in thermal energy of the **water**.

Use the correct equation from the Physics Equation Sheet.

Increase in thermal energy of water = ... J **[2 marks]**

07.2 The temperature of the metal block decreases by 70°C

The mass of the block is 0.10 kg

The specific heat capacity of the block is 500 J/kg °C

Calculate the **decrease** in thermal energy of the **metal block**.

Use the correct equation from the Physics Equation Sheet.

Decrease in thermal energy of metal block = ... J **[2 marks]**

07.3 Suggest **one** reason why the **increase** in thermal energy of the water is less than the **decrease** in thermal energy of the block.

....

[1 mark]

08   The resistance of a particular type of wire depends on its length and its thickness.

A student decides to investigate how the resistance of a wire depends on its length.

08.1   Identify the **independent variable**, the **dependent variable** and the **control variable** in this investigation.

Independent variable: ....

Dependent variable: ....

Control variable: ....   **[3 marks]**

08.2   **Figure 8.1** shows a circuit that can be used to determine the resistance of a length of wire.

The wire under test is connected between crocodile clips **X** and **Y**.

Describe how the student could use this circuit in their investigation.

Include any additional apparatus that you think the student may need.

Figure 8.1

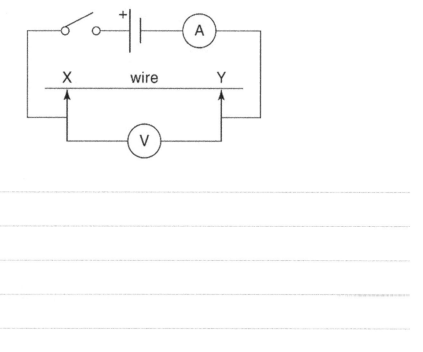

....

....

....

....

....

....

....

                                                                                                         [4 marks]

Question 8 continues on the next page

08.3 The student decides to take repeat measurements for each length of wire.

What type of error does the repeat of measurements help to reduce?

Tick **one** box.

Zero error ☐

Systematic error ☐

Random error ☐ **[1 mark]**

08.4 The resistance of the student's wire is directly proportional to its length.

Sketch a graph on the axes in **Figure 8.2** to show how the resistance of the wire depends on its length.

Figure 8.2

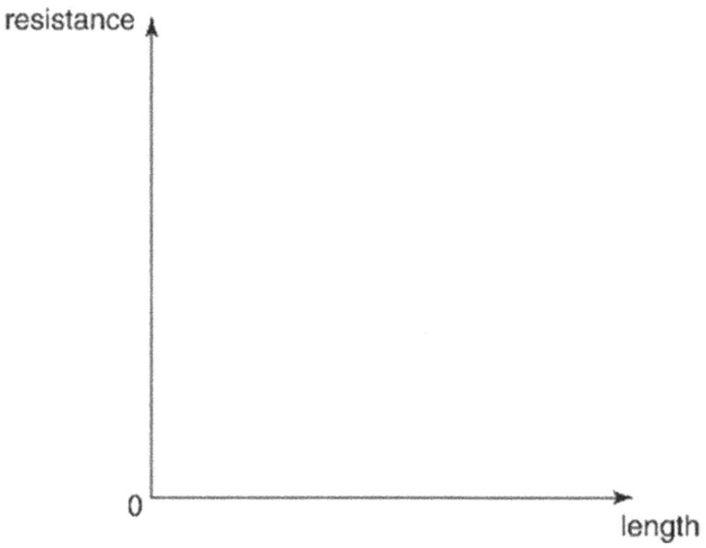

[1 mark]

08.5 The resistance of a 1.00 m length of wire is 11 Ω

The resistance of the wire is directly proportional to its length.

Calculate the length of a piece of this wire that would have a resistance of 2.2 Ω

Length = _____ m **[2 marks]**

09   In the particle model of matter, particles are sometimes shown as small circles.

09.1 Draw particles in the box to show the particle model of a **gas**.

[1 mark]

09.2 Describe the motion of the gas particles.

....

.... [2 marks]

09.3 Give the term that is used to describe the total kinetic energy and potential energy of all of the particles in a gas?

.... [1 mark]

09.4 Which **two** of the following statements correctly describe the behaviour of a gas heated at a constant volume?

Tick **two** boxes.

Increasing the temperature increases the speed of
the gas particles.   ☐

Increasing the temperature decreases the average
kinetic energy of the gas particles.   ☐

Increasing the temperature decreases the
gas pressure.   ☐

Increasing the temperature increases the
gas pressure.   ☐   [2 marks]

Question 9 continues on the next page

09.5 **Figure 9.1(a)** shows a gas-filled cylinder.

It is sealed by a moveable piston.

Figure 9.1

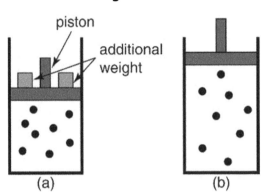

The pressure of the gas is 200 000 Pa

The volume occupied by the gas is initially 2000 cm³

The temperature of the gas is 20°C

When the additional weights are slowly removed, the piston moves upwards and comes to a stop (**Figure 9.1(b)**).

The new volume of the gas is 2500 cm³

The temperature of the gas is still 20°C

Calculate the new pressure of the gas.

Use the correct equation from the Physics Equation Sheet.

New pressure = _____ Pa **[3 marks]**

10 The circuit diagram in **Figure 10.1** has three **identical** resistors.

Figure 10.1

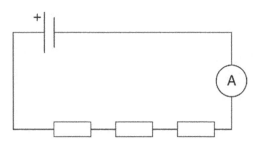

10.1 Which **two** statements about the circuit are correct?

Tick **two** boxes.

The potential difference across each resistor has the same value. ☐

The resistors are connected in parallel. ☐

The current through each resistor has a different value. ☐

The resistors are connected in series. ☐ **[2 marks]**

10.2 Each of the resistors in the circuit has a resistance of 5.0 Ω

Calculate the total resistance of the three resistors in the circuit.

_____

Total resistance = _____ Ω **[1 mark]**

10.3 Write down the equation that links potential difference, current and resistance.

_____ **[1 mark]**

10.4 The cell in the circuit of **Figure 10.1** supplies a potential difference of 1.5 V

Calculate the size of the electric current in the circuit.

_____

Current = _____ A **[3 marks]**

Question 10 continues on the next page

10.5 Write down the equation that links charge, current and time.

.... **[1 mark]**

10.6 Calculate the charge that flows around the circuit in 5 minutes.

....

....

Charge = ... C   **[3 marks]**

10.7 Each of the resistors in the circuit can be described as an ohmic conductor.

Explain what is meant by an **ohmic conductor**.

....

.... **[1 mark]**

10.8 A diode is an electrical component that is **not** an ohmic conductor.

Draw the circuit symbol for a diode in the box below.

[1 mark]

10.9 **Figure 10.2** shows how the current through a diode changes with the potential difference across it.

Figure 10.2

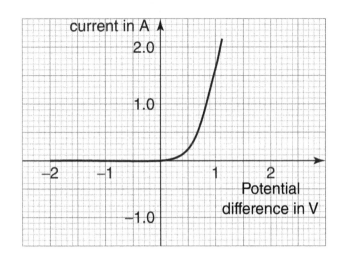

Write down **two** things that the graph shows about how a diode works.

1. ....

2. .... **[2 marks]**

Turn over >

11.1 The main sources of energy used in UK power stations are listed in this box.

natural gas	wood	uranium	coal
solar	wind	hydroelectric	oil

Complete the following sentences.

Choose words from the box.

.... is an example of a biofuel.

.... is an example of a fossil fuel. **[2 marks]**

11.2 A power station transfers energy from an input energy source to generate electricity as output energy.

Write down the equation for calculating the **efficiency** of an energy transfer process.

....

.... **[1 mark]**

11.3 A gas power station generates electrical power at 720 MW

Natural gas supplies energy to the power station at a rate of 1200 MW

Calculate the efficiency of the power station.

....

....

Efficiency = ... **[2 marks]**

11.4 Wind turbines and coal-fuelled power stations are both used to generate electricity in the UK.

Compare the advantages and disadvantages of wind turbines and coal-fuelled power stations for generating electricity in the UK.

Include comparisons of their **reliability** and **environmental effects**.

_____

_____

_____

_____

_____

_____

_____

_____

_____

_____

_____

_____

_____

_____

_____

[6 marks]

END OF QUESTIONS

Physics Equation Sheet

Equation Number	Word Equation	Symbol Equation
1	(final velocity)^2 – (initial velocity)^2 = 2 × acceleration × distance	$v^2 - u^2 = 2\,a\,s$
2	elastic potential energy = 0.5 × spring constant × (extension)^2	$E_e = \dfrac{1}{2}\,ke^2$
3	change in thermal energy = mass × specific heat capacity × temperature change	$\Delta E = m\,c\,\Delta\theta$
4	period = $\dfrac{1}{\text{frequency}}$	
5	magnification = $\dfrac{\text{image height}}{\text{object height}}$	
6	thermal energy for a change of state = mass × specific latent heat	$E = m\,L$
7	potential difference across primary coil × current in primary coil = potential difference across secondary coil × current in secondary coil	$V_p I_p = V_s I_s$
8	For gases: pressure × volume = constant	$pV = \text{constant}$

Collins

AQA

GCSE

PHYSICS

F

SET A – Paper 2 Foundation Tier

Author: Lynn Pharaoh

Time allowed: 1 hour 45 minutes

Materials

For this paper you must have: • a ruler   • a calculator.   • the Physics Equation Sheet (found at the end of the paper).

Instructions

- Answer **all** questions in the spaces provided.
- Do all rough work in this book. Cross through any work you do not want to be marked.

Information

- There are 100 marks available on this paper.
- The marks for questions are shown in brackets.
- You are expected to use a calculator where appropriate.
- You are reminded of the need for good English and clear presentation in your answers.
- When answering questions 04.5 and 09.1 you need to make sure that your answer:
  - is clear, logical, sensibly structured
  - fully meets the requirements of the question
  - shows that each separate point or step supports the overall answer.

Advice

- In all calculations, show clearly how you work out your answer.

Name: ....

01.1 Give the name of the force that pulls gas and dust together to start the formation of a star.

.... **[1 mark]**

01.2 **Figure 1.1** shows some of the stages in the life cycle of a star that is about the **same size** as the Sun.

Figure 1.1

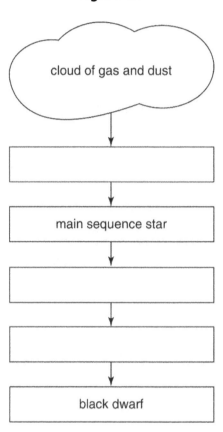

Complete **Figure 1.1** by writing the names of the 3 missing stages for such a star.

[3 marks]

01.3 The two sketch graphs in **Figure 1.2** show information about **main sequence** stars.

Figure 1.2

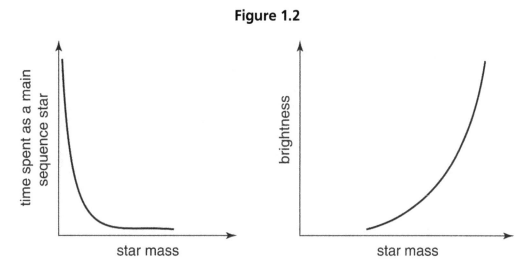

star mass

star mass

Using information from the graphs, complete the following sentences.

Choose words from the box.

greater	smaller	the same as

A A high-mass star spends a .... amount of time as a main sequence star than a low-mass star spends as a main sequence star.

B The brightness of a high-mass star is .... than the brightness of a low-mass star.

[2 marks]

Turn over >

02   **Figure 2.1** shows a plan view of a ripple tank used to investigate the behaviour of waves.

Figure 2.1

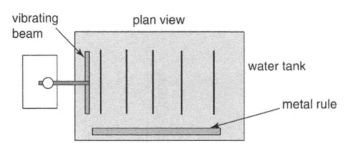

02.1 The vibrating beam in the ripple tank produces waves which travel across the tank.

The beam makes 20 waves in 4 s

What is the frequency of the waves?

Tick **one** box.

20 Hz   ☐

5.0 Hz   ☐

80 Hz   ☐   **[1 mark]**

02.2 The parallel lines on the ripple tank in **Figure 2.1** represent lines of wave crests.

What is the name given to the distance from one line of crests to the next line of crests?

Tick **one** box.

wavelength   ☐

amplitude   ☐

speed   ☐   **[1 mark]**

02.3 The frequency of the waves on the ripple tank is changed to 3.0 Hz

The wavelength of the waves is measured at 4.0 cm

Calculate the speed of these ripple tank waves.

Use the following equation.

speed = frequency × wavelength

Wave speed = _____ cm/s **[2 marks]**

02.4 A student investigates how the speed of a wave on water varies with the depth of the water in the tank.

Identify the **independent** variable and the **dependent** variable.

Independent variable: _____

Dependent variable: _____ **[2 marks]**

Question 2 continues on the next page

02.5 Figure 2.2 is a sketch graph of the student's results.

Figure 2.2

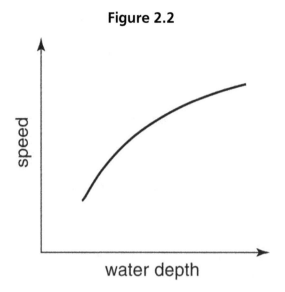

Which **two** statements are correct conclusions to the data shown in **Figure 2.2**?

Tick **two** boxes.

The wave travels faster in deeper water. ☐

The wave travels slower in deeper water. ☐

Wave speed increases steadily as the water gets deeper. ☐

Wave speed is not directly proportional to depth of water. ☐   **[2 marks]**

03.1 Which **two** of these quantities have both magnitude and direction?

Tick **two** boxes.

force ☐

distance ☐

speed ☐

displacement ☐   **[2 marks]**

03.2 **Figure 3.1** represents the motion of a car on a straight road.

Figure 3.1

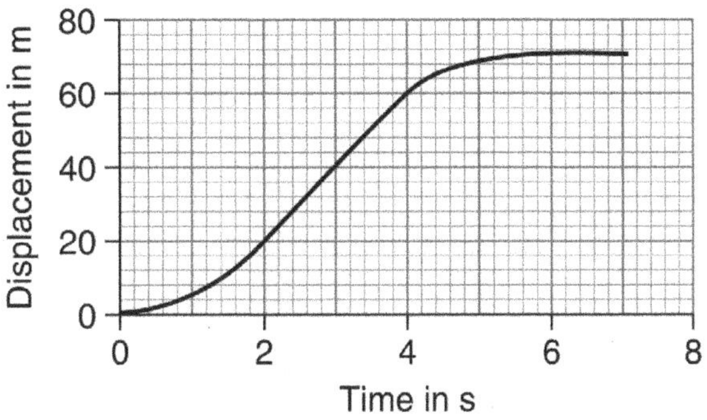

Use **Figure 3.1** to give **three** conclusions about the car's journey.

1. ....

....

2. ....

....

3. ....

.... **[3 marks]**

Question 3 continues on the next page

03.3 Use **Figure 3.1** to determine the displacement of the car at 4 s

Distance = _____ m   **[1 mark]**

03.4 Calculate the average speed of the car during the first 4 s of its motion.

Use the following equation.

$$\text{average speed} = \frac{\text{distance}}{\text{time}}$$

Average speed = _____ m/s   **[2 marks]**

04.1 Complete the following sentences about magnets.

Use the terms from the box below.

| an attractive force | a repulsive force | no force |

The north pole of a magnet exerts _____ on the south pole of another magnet.

The north pole of a magnet exerts _____ on a piece of magnetic material such as iron.

The north pole of a magnet exerts _____ on the north pole of another magnet.

The south pole of a magnet exerts _____ on the south pole of another magnet.

[4 marks]

04.2 Which description of the magnetic force between two magnets is correct?

Tick **one** box.

A contact force ☐

A non-contact force ☐

[1 mark]

04.3 Describe the differences between a **permanent magnet** and an **induced magnet**.

_____

_____

_____

_____

[2 marks]

Question 4 continues on the next page

04.4 **Figure 4.1** shows two magnetic field lines in the space around a bar magnet.

Add an arrow to **each** of the field lines to show the direction of the magnetic field.

Figure 4.1

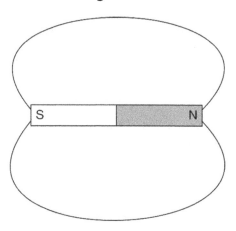

[2 marks]

04.5 Write a set of instructions for plotting a magnetic field line around a bar magnet using a compass.

You may include a diagram as part of your answer.

[4 marks]

05.1 Which **two** statements represent Newton's first law of motion correctly?

Tick **two** boxes.

The resultant force on a stationary object is zero. ☐

Acceleration is proportional to resultant force. ☐

When two objects exert forces on each other, the forces are equal and opposite. ☐

The resultant force on an object moving at a steady speed is zero. ☐ **[2 marks]**

05.2 **Figure 5.1** shows a van travelling along a straight road.

The arrows represent the forces acting on the van.

Figure 5.1

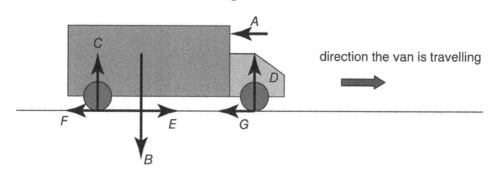

direction the van is travelling

Which arrow in **Figure 5.1** represents the driving force created by the van's engine?

Tick **one** box.

A	B	C	D	E	F	G

[1 mark]

05.3 Which **two** forces shown in **Figure 5.1** represent friction between the tyres and the road?

Tick **two** boxes.

A	B	C	D	E	F	G

[2 marks]

Question 5 continues on the next page

05.4 The van in **Figure 5.1** is travelling at a velocity of 10 m/s

The van now accelerates to a velocity of 14 m/s

It takes 2.5 s to reach a velocity of 14 m/s

Use the following equation to calculate the van's acceleration.

$$\text{acceleration} = \frac{\text{change in velocity}}{\text{time}}$$

Give the correct unit with your answer.

Acceleration = ...

Unit: .... **[3 marks]**

05.5 Write down the equation that links resultant force, mass and acceleration.

[1 mark]

05.6 The mass of the van is 4000 kg

Calculate the resultant force acting on the van while it is accelerating.

Resultant force = ... N **[2 marks]**

05.7 The driving force from the van's engine during the acceleration is 8000 N

Calculate the total resistive force acting on the van during the acceleration.

Resistive force = ... N **[2 marks]**

06.1 Explain what causes air to exert a force on a surface.

.... **[1 mark]**

06.2 Write down the equation that links pressure to normal force and surface area.

.... **[1 mark]**

06.3 Atmospheric pressure at sea level is 100 000 Pa

The average surface area of an adult human is 1.8 m²

Calculate the force exerted by the atmosphere on the surface of an adult human.

....

....

Force = ... N **[3 marks]**

06.4 **Figure 6.1** shows the variation of atmospheric pressure with height.

Figure 6.1

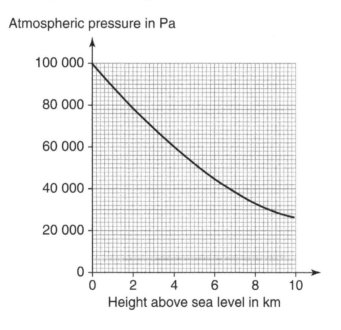

Write down a conclusion you can make from the graph.

....

.... **[1 mark]**

Question 6 continues on the next page

06.5 A student suggests that atmospheric pressure **halves** when height above sea level **doubles**.

Use data from the graph in **Figure 6.1** to show whether or not the student's suggestion is correct.

....

....

....

.... **[3 marks]**

06.6 Explain why the pressure exerted by the atmosphere on a person is greatest at sea level.

....

....

.... **[2 marks]**

07.1 **Figure 7.1** shows 3 parallel rays of light incident on a convex lens.

Draw in the paths of the three rays after they pass through the lens.

Mark with the letter **F** the position of the **principal focus** of the lens.

Figure 7.1

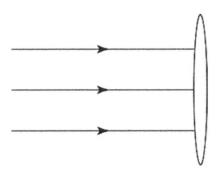

[4 marks]

07.2 Define the term **focal length**.

....

.... [1 mark]

07.3 A convex lens is set up to produce an image of an illuminated object on a screen.

Figure 7.2 shows an incomplete ray diagram of the set-up.

O represents the object.

Figure 7.2

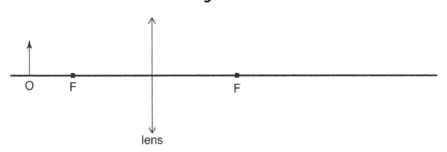

Complete the ray diagram to show the formation of the image on the right hand side of the lens.

Draw **two** rays from the object to do this.

Mark the image I.

[3 marks]

Question 7 continues on the next page

07.4 A student uses the apparatus in **Figure 7.3** to produce an image of a cross-wire on a screen.

The position of the screen is adjusted to produce a clear, focused image.

Figure 7.3

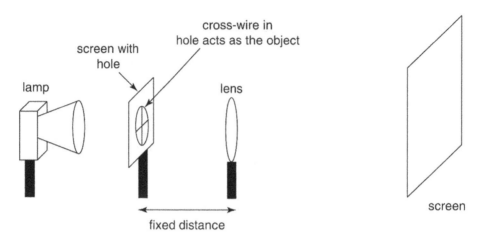

Figure 7.4 shows the appearance of the image on the screen.

Figure 7.4

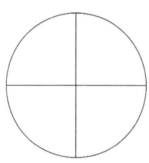

Describe how the student could measure the **magnification** produced by the lens.

Include any additional apparatus that the student may need.

....

....

....

....

....

....

[4 marks]

07.5 The student wants to find out if the focal length of a convex lens affects its magnification.

The student uses the apparatus shown in **Figure 7.3** with three convex lenses in turn.

Each lens has a different focal length.

During the experiment, she keeps the distance from the object to the lens fixed.

Table 7.1 shows her results.

Table 7.1

Focal length in mm	Object height in mm	Image height in mm	Magnification
100	20	20	1.0
120	20	30	1.5
150	20	60	

Write the missing magnification value in the table.

Use the equation for magnification from the Physics Equation Sheet.

[1 mark]

07.6 Give **one** conclusion that can be made from the data in **Table 7.1**

....

....

[1 mark]

07.7 The student wants to learn more about the way that focal length affects the magnification.

Suggest improvements to the experiment and the analysis of the data that could achieve this.

....

....

....

....

[3 marks]

Turn over >

08   **Figure 8.1** is a plan view of a door.

Pulling the door handle causes the door to open by rotating about its hinges.

Figure 8.1

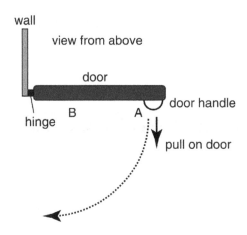

08.1 Explain why it is easier to open the door by pulling at position A rather than pulling at position B.

[2 marks]

....

....

....

08.2 Write down the equation which links moment, force and distance.

[1 mark]

....

08.3 The door handle is 75 cm from the hinge.

A person pulls with a force of 2.0 N on the door handle.

Calculate the size of the clockwise moment exerted on the door.

Give your answer in N m.

[3 marks]

....

....

Moment = ... N m

08.4 **Figure 8.2** shows a stationary wheelbarrow.

A gardener is applying an upward force to the handle of the wheelbarrow.

This holds the back legs of the wheelbarrow just off the ground.

Figure 8.2

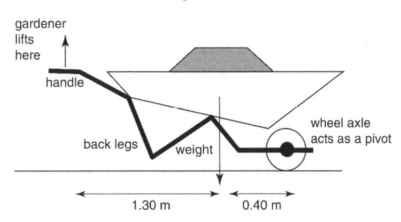

The front wheel of the wheelbarrow acts as a pivot.

Complete the following sentence.

Choose from **a clockwise moment** or **an anticlockwise moment**.

The total weight of the wheelbarrow and its load creates

....   **[1 mark]**

08.5 The total weight of the wheelbarrow and its load is 200 N

Calculate the size of the moment due to the total weight.

Take the front wheel as the pivot.

....

....

Moment = ... N m **[2 marks]**

08.6 Give the direction of the moment produced by the force exerted by the gardener.

.... **[1 mark]**

Question 8 continues on the next page

08.7 Give the size of the moment produced by the gardener to keep the wheelbarrow balanced.

Take the front wheel as the pivot.

Moment = ... N m   **[1 mark]**

08.8 Calculate the upward force that the gardener must exert to keep the wheelbarrow balanced with its back legs just off the ground.

Give your answer to 2 significant figures.

Force = ... N   **[3 marks]**

09.1 A student is asked to use the apparatus in **Figure 9.1** to obtain a series of measurements of the extension of a spring.

She has a range of standard weights to attach to the spring.

Figure 9.1

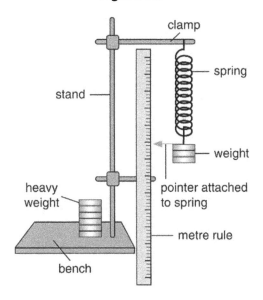

Write a set of instructions that the student could follow to obtain the measurements as accurately as possible.

....

....

....

....

....

....

....

....

....

....

.... **[6 marks]**

Question 9 continues on the next page

09.2 The student repeats the experiment for two more springs.

Data for the three springs, **A**, **B** and **C**, are displayed on the graph in **Figure 9.2**

Figure 9.2

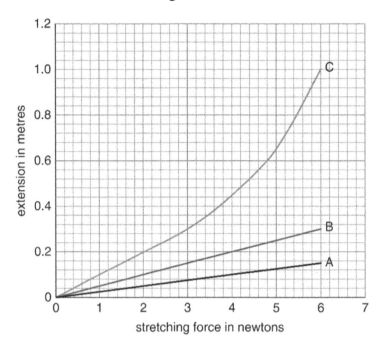

Which one of the springs has been stretched beyond its limit of proportionality?

Tick **one** box.

A ☐

B ☐

C ☐

[1 mark]

09.3 Which is the stiffest spring?

Tick **one** box.

A ☐

B ☐

C ☐

[1 mark]

09.4 Which of the springs is the easiest to stretch?

Tick **one** box.

A ☐

B ☐

C ☐

[1 mark]

09.5 Which one of the springs requires a force of 4.0 N to extend it by 0.20 m?

A ☐

B ☐

C ☐

[1 mark]

END OF QUESTIONS

Physics Equation Sheet

Equation Number	Word Equation	Symbol Equation
1	(final velocity)^2 – (initial velocity)^2 = 2 × acceleration × distance	$v^2 - u^2 = 2\,a\,s$
2	elastic potential energy = 0.5 × spring constant × (extension)^2	$E_e = \dfrac{1}{2}\,ke^2$
3	change in thermal energy = mass × specific heat capacity × temperature change	$\Delta E = m\,c\,\Delta\theta$
4	period = $\dfrac{1}{\text{frequency}}$	
5	magnification = $\dfrac{\text{image height}}{\text{object height}}$	
6	thermal energy for a change of state = mass × specific latent heat	$E = m\,L$
7	potential difference across primary coil × current in primary coil = potential difference across secondary coil × current in secondary coil	$V_p I_p = V_s I_s$
8	For gases: pressure × volume = constant	$pV = \text{constant}$

©HarperCollins*Publishers* 2019

Collins

AQA

GCSE

PHYSICS

F

SET B – Paper 1 Foundation Tier

Author: Lynn Pharaoh

Time allowed: 1 hour 45 minutes

Materials

For this paper you must have:

- a ruler
- a calculator.
- the Physics Equation Sheet (found at the end of the paper).

Instructions

- Answer **all** questions in the spaces provided.
- Do all rough work in this book. Cross through any work you do not want to be marked.

Information

- There are 100 marks available on this paper.
- The marks for questions are shown in brackets.
- You are expected to use a calculator where appropriate.
- You are reminded of the need for good English and clear presentation in your answers.
- When answering questions 06 and 12.2 you need to make sure that your answer:
  – is clear, logical, sensibly structured
  – fully meets the requirements of the question
  – shows that each separate point or step supports the overall answer.

Advice

- In all calculations, show clearly how you work out your answer.

Name: ....

01.1 Which type of nuclear radiation has the **greatest ionising power**?

Tick **one** box.

Alpha ☐

Beta ☐

Gamma ☐

[1 mark]

01.2 Which type of nuclear radiation has the **longest range in air**?

Tick **one** box.

Alpha ☐

Beta ☐

Gamma ☐

[1 mark]

01.3 Which type of nuclear radiation consists of **high speed electrons**?

Tick **one** box.

Alpha ☐

Beta ☐

Gamma ☐

[1 mark]

01.4 Which type of nuclear radiation does **not** consist of **charged particles**?

Tick **one** box.

Alpha ☐

Beta ☐

Gamma ☐

[1 mark]

01.5 Which type of nuclear radiation is **not** suitable for medical **exploration of internal organs**?

Tick **one** box.

Alpha ☐

Beta ☐

Gamma ☐

[1 mark]

01.6 Which type of nuclear radiation consists of **two protons** and **two neutrons**?

Tick **one** box.

Alpha ☐

Beta ☐

Gamma ☐

[1 mark]

Turn over >

02   A student wants to investigate how the thickness of bubble wrap affects its thermal insulation properties.

Figure 2.1 shows the apparatus that the student uses.

Figure 2.1

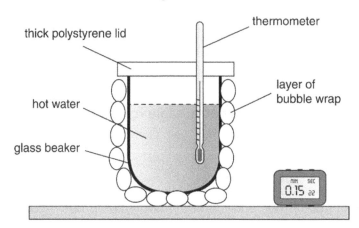

02.1 The student uses a volume of 100 cm³ of hot water in the beaker.

He measures the time taken for the temperature of the hot water in the beaker to fall by 20°C, from 80°C to 60°C

He records time measurements for 1, 2, 3, and 4 layers of bubble wrap.

Identify **two control variables** in this investigation.

1. ....

2. ....   **[2 marks]**

02.2 **Table 2.1** shows the student's measurements.

Table 2.1

Number of layers of bubble wrap	Time in seconds for temperature drop
1	220
2	340
3	440
4	560

Use the data in **Table 2.1** to help you to complete the sentences below.

Choose from the words in the box.

increases	decreases

Increasing the number of layers of bubble wrap around the beaker

.... the time taken for the temperature to drop from
80°C to 60°C

Increasing the number of layers of bubble wrap around the beaker

.... the thermal energy transferred to the surroundings
each second.   **[2 marks]**

Question 2 continues on the next page

02.3 Figure 2.2 shows the student's data displayed in a bar chart.

Figure 2.2

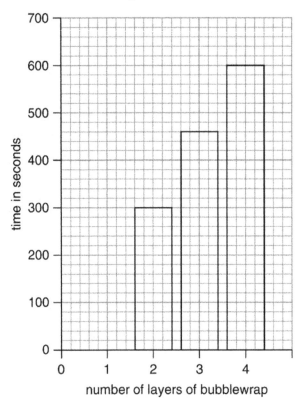

The bar chart is incomplete.

Add the missing data.

[1 mark]

02.4 Table 2.2 shows the thermal conductivity of three insulating materials.

Table 2.2

Material	Thermal conductivity in W/(m K)
Expanded polystyrene	0.03
Glass wool	0.04
Rock wool	0.045

Which material listed in **Table 2.2** is the **best thermal insulator**?

[1 mark]

03.1 Write down what is meant by a **renewable** energy source.

....

.... **[1 mark]**

03.2 Give an example of a renewable energy source that is used to generate electricity.

.... **[1 mark]**

03.3 In the UK, a system of cables and transformers links power stations to consumers.

What is the name of this system?

.... **[1 mark]**

Question 3 continues on the next page

03.4 In UK homes, cables that connect a mains socket to an appliance contain three wires with different colour schemes.

Draw a line from **each** wire to its colour scheme.

wire	colour scheme

wire
Live
Neutral
Earth

colour scheme
blue
Green and yellow stripes
brown

[2 marks]

03.5 Which wire prevents the appliance from becoming live if there is a fault?

Tick **one** box.

Live ☐

Neutral ☐

Earth ☐

[1 mark]

03.6 The potential difference supplied by the mains in the UK is 230 V

When a toaster is plugged into the mains it draws an electric current of 3.0 A

Use the following equation to calculate the power of the toaster:

power = potential difference × current

Give the correct unit with your answer.

Power = ...

Unit: .... [3 marks]

04.1 What is the approximate radius of an atom?

Tick **one** box.

1×10^{-2} m ☐

1×10^{-5} m ☐

1×10^{-10} m ☐ [1 mark]

04.2 Experiments during the late 19th century and the early 20th century enabled scientists to develop the model of the atom.

They replaced the **plum pudding model** with the **nuclear model**.

Describe the main features of the plum pudding model of the atom.

....

....

....
[2 marks]

04.3 Describe the main features of the nuclear model of the atom.

....

....

....
[2 marks]

04.4 Further experiments showed that the atomic nucleus consists of two types of particle.

Name the **two** types of particle found in the nucleus.

1. ....

2. ....
[2 marks]

05   A system is an object or a group of objects.

The way energy is stored in a system can change when the system changes.

05.1   Draw a line from **each** system change to the correct energy store change.

System change	Energy store change
	Gravitational potential energy to kinetic energy
A cup of tea cooling down	Elastic potential energy to thermal energy
A falling football	Thermal energy dissipated to the surroundings
A car braking	Kinetic energy to thermal energy
	Thermal energy to kinetic energy

[3 marks]

05.2   A student attaches a weight to a spring, causing the spring to stretch.

Name the energy store associated with the stretched spring.

[1 mark]

05.3   The weight extends the spring by 0.12 m

The spring constant of the spring is 25 N/m

Calculate the amount of energy stored in the spring.

Use the following equation.

$$\text{energy stored} = \frac{1}{2} \times \text{spring constant} \times (\text{extension})^2$$

Energy stored = _____ J   [2 marks]

06.1 A student uses the set-up in **Figure 6.1** to demonstrate the following to her class:

Two objects that carry the same type of charge repel

Two objects that carry different types of charge attract

The materials she has are:

- a piece of cloth
- two acetate rods
- two polythene rods

The apparatus that she has allows a rod to be suspended so that it can rotate freely.

Figure 6.1

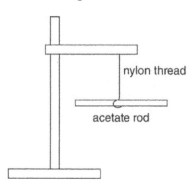

The student knows that:

- polythene can gain a negative charge, and
- acetate can gain a positive charge.

Describe the demonstration that she should carry out.

....

....

....

....

....

....

....

....

[4 marks]

Turn over >

07.1 Figure 7.1 shows the main sources of background radiation at a specific location.

Figure 7.1

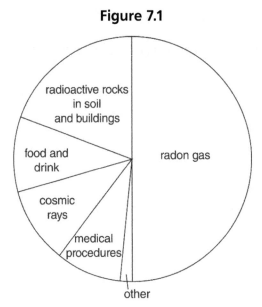

Typical contribution of different sources to background radiation

What are the **two largest sources** of background radiation at this location?

1. ....

2. ....   **[2 marks]**

07.2 **Table 7.1** contains information about radon gas doses.

Table 7.1

Location	Dose in mSv
Annual average radon dose across the UK	1.3
Annual average radon dose in Cornwall	6.9

[Data from Public Health England]

Calculate **how many times greater** the radon dose is in Cornwall compared with the average dose across the UK.

Number of times greater = _____ **[1 mark]**

07.3 A nucleus of an isotope of radon, $^{222}_{86}$Rn, undergoes radioactive decay by alpha emission to form a nucleus of polonium, Po.

Complete the nuclear equation showing the decay of radon-222

Add the **two** missing numbers to the equation.

$$^{222}_{86}\text{Rn} \rightarrow \,^{218}_{}\text{Po} + \,_{2}\text{He}$$

[2 marks]

07.4 The polonium-218 nucleus undergoes radioactive decay by beta emission.

Complete the nuclear equation showing the decay of polonium-218

Add the **three** missing numbers to the equation.

$$^{218}_{84}\text{Po} \rightarrow \,_{}\text{At} + \,^{0}_{}\text{e}$$

[3 marks]

08.1 **Figure 8.1** shows a uranium nucleus undergoing fission.

Figure 8.1

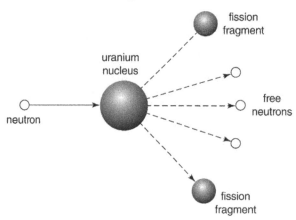

Describe what must happen for a chain reaction to start in a sample of uranium.

....

.... **[2 marks]**

08.2 What type of energy store do the products of the fission event have?

Tick **one** box.

Chemical ☐

Kinetic ☐

Sound ☐ **[1 mark]**

08.3 Give an example of where an **uncontrolled** fission chain reaction occurs.

.... **[1 mark]**

08.4 When a uranium nucleus undergoes fission it splits into smaller nuclei called fission fragments (**Figure 8.1**).

The fission fragments are unstable and undergo radioactive decay.

The fission fragments produced in a nuclear reactor form radioactive waste.

Table 8.1 lists some fission fragments and their half-life values.

Table 8.1

Fission fragment	Half-life
Barium-140	12 days
Caesium-137	30 years
Iodine-131	8 days
Krypton-85	11 years
Xenon-140	14 s

Which **two** fission fragments will need to be stored safely for hundreds of years?

1. ....

2. .... [2 marks]

08.5 Explain your answer to question 08.4

....

....

.... [3 marks]

08.6 **Figure 8.2** shows a proton colliding with a deuteron and creating a nucleus of an isotope of helium.

Figure 8.2

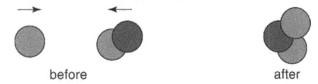

before   after

What is the name of the process shown in **Figure 8.2**?

.... [1 mark]

Turn over >

09 The specific heat capacity of a material can be measured by heating the material with an electrical heater.

09.1 Explain what is meant by **specific heat capacity**.

[1 mark]

....

....

09.2 **Figure 9.1** shows apparatus used to determine the specific heat capacity of an aluminium block.

The joulemeter shows the amount of electrical energy supplied to the block over a specific amount of time.

Figure 9.1

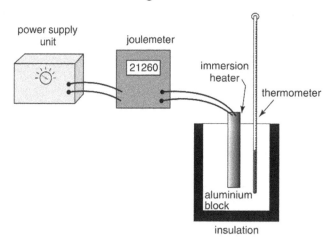

The temperature of the block needs to be recorded before and after it is heated.

The temperature of the block is expected to rise by approximately 20°C

The room temperature of the laboratory is about 18°C

Table 9.1 lists some thermometers that are available.

Table 9.1

Thermometer	Range in °C	Value of one division in °C
A	−10 to 110	1
B	34 to 44	0.1
C	−10 to 50	0.5
D	−10 to 200	2

Choose the most suitable thermometer for the experiment.

Explain your answer.

Thermometer: ....

....

....

....

.... **[3 marks]**

09.3 Measurements taken using the apparatus in **Figure 9.1** are shown in **Table 9.2**

Table 9.2

Measurement	Value
Initial temperature of the block	18.5°C
Final temperature of the block	41.5°C
Energy supplied	21260 J
Mass of block	1.00 kg

Determine the specific heat capacity of aluminium.

Use the correct equation from the Physics Equation Sheet.

Give your answer to 3 significant figures.

....

....

....

Specific heat capacity = ... J/kg °C **[5 marks]**

Turn over >

10.1 Name component **Q** in **Figure 10.1**

Figure 10.1

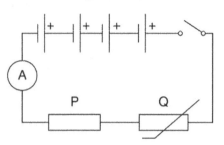

[1 mark]

10.2 Figure 10.2 shows how the resistance of component **Q** changes as its temperature is changed.

Figure 10.2

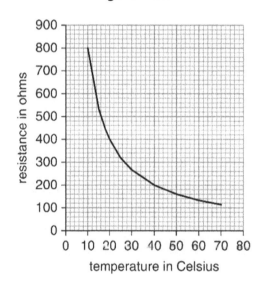

Describe the trend shown by **Figure 10.2**

[1 mark]

10.3 Explain how the reading on the ammeter in **Figure 10.1** would change if the temperature of component **Q** increased.

[2 marks]

©HarperCollins*Publishers* 2019

10.4 Use **Figure 10.2** to determine the resistance of component **Q** at temperature of 20°C

Resistance = _____ Ω   **[1 mark]**

10.5 Component **P** in the circuit of **Figure 10.1** is a fixed resistor of resistance of 800 Ω

Calculate the **total resistance** in the circuit when component **Q** is at 20°C

_____

Total resistance = _____ Ω   **[1 mark]**

10.6 Write down the equation that links potential difference, current and resistance.

_____   **[1 mark]**

10.7 The battery in **Figure 10.1** supplies a potential difference of 6.0 V

Calculate the current through the ammeter when component **Q** is at 20°C

_____

_____

Current = _____ A   **[3 marks]**

10.8 Write down the equation that links power, current and resistance.

_____   **[1 mark]**

10.9 Calculate the power transferred by resistor **P**.

Give your answer in milliwatts.

_____

Power = _____ mW   **[3 marks]**

Turn over >

11 A student sets up a circuit to measure current and potential difference values for an unknown electrical component.

Figure 11.1 shows the component marked with an 'X'.

Figure 11.1

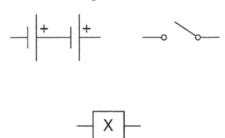

11.1 A circuit is needed that allows **several different** measurements to be taken of current through **X** and potential difference across **X**.

Complete the circuit diagram in **Figure 11.1** to show a suitable circuit. **[3 marks]**

11.2 Write down the equation that links charge, current and time.

[1 mark]

11.3 The student sets up the circuit so that the current is 0.12 A

Calculate the charge that flows through component **X** in 10 s

Charge = _____ C **[2 marks]**

11.4 Write down the equation that links energy transferred with charge flow and potential difference.

[1 mark]

11.5 When the current is 0.12 A, the student measures the potential difference across **X** to be 0.60 V

Calculate the energy transferred by component **X** in 10 s

Energy transferred = _____ J [2 marks]

11.6 **Figure 11.2** is a graph of the student's current and potential difference measurements for component **X**.

Figure 11.2

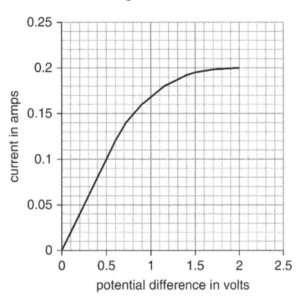

Explain how the resistance of the component varies as the potential difference is increased.

_____

_____

_____

[3 marks]

12.1 **Table 12.1** shows the density of liquid water and water vapour.

Table 12.1

State of water	Density in g/cm³
Liquid	0.998
Vapour (steam)	0.590

Explain what can be concluded from **Table 12.1** about the arrangement of molecules in liquid water compared with water vapour.

[3 marks]

12.2 A student is asked to measure the density of cooking oil.

Describe a plan for the student to follow.

Name any apparatus to be used.

[6 marks]

END OF QUESTIONS

BLANK PAGE

Physics Equation Sheet

Equation Number	Word Equation	Symbol Equation
1	(final velocity)^2 – (initial velocity)^2 = 2 × acceleration × distance	$v^2 - u^2 = 2\,a\,s$
2	elastic potential energy = 0.5 × spring constant × (extension)^2	$E_e = \dfrac{1}{2}\,ke^2$
3	change in thermal energy = mass × specific heat capacity × temperature change	$\Delta E = m\,c\,\Delta\theta$
4	period = $\dfrac{1}{\text{frequency}}$	
5	magnification = $\dfrac{\text{image height}}{\text{object height}}$	
6	thermal energy for a change of state = mass × specific latent heat	$E = m\,L$
7	potential difference across primary coil × current in primary coil = potential difference across secondary coil × current in secondary coil	$V_p I_p = V_s I_s$
8	For gases: pressure × volume = constant	pV = constant

Collins

AQA

GCSE

PHYSICS

F

SET B – Paper 2 Foundation Tier

Author: Lynn Pharaoh

Time allowed: 1 hour 45 minutes

Materials

For this paper you must have:

- a ruler
- a calculator.
- the Physics Equation Sheet (found at the end of the paper).

Instructions

- Answer **all** questions in the spaces provided.
- Do all rough work in this book. Cross through any work you do not want to be marked.

Information

- There are 100 marks available on this paper.
- The marks for questions are shown in brackets.
- You are expected to use a calculator where appropriate.
- You are reminded of the need for good English and clear presentation in your answers.
- When answering questions 08.3 and 11 you need to make sure that your answer:
  - is clear, logical, sensibly structured
  - fully meets the requirements of the question
  - shows that each separate point or step supports the overall answer.

Advice

- In all calculations, show clearly how you work out your answer.

Name: ....

01.1 **Figure 1.1** shows some of the stages in the life cycle of a star **many times more massive** than the Sun.

Figure 1.1

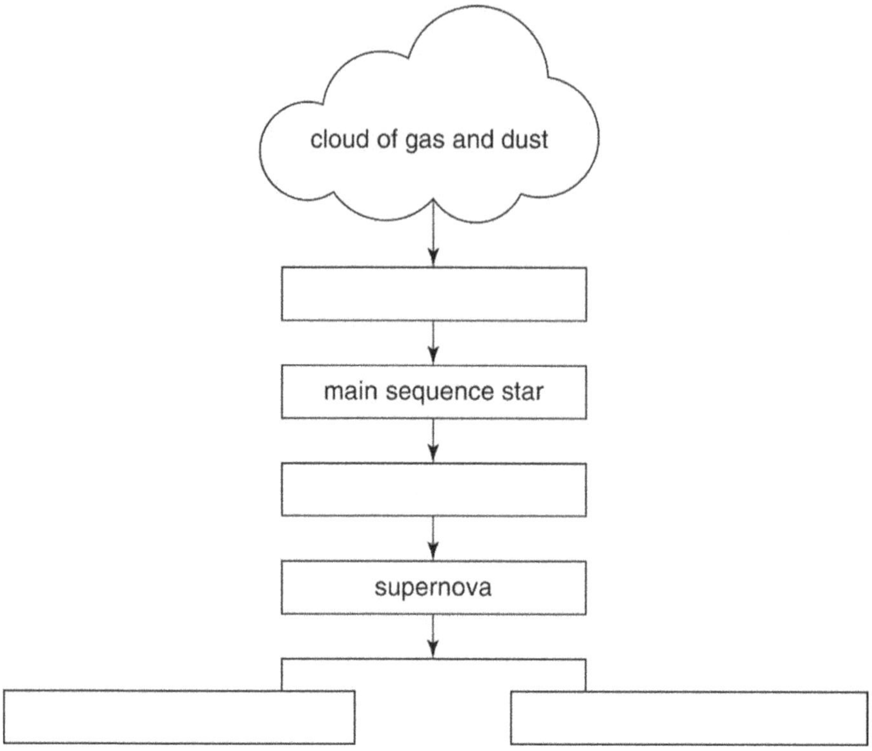

```
        ╭───────────────────╮
       (  cloud of gas and dust )
        ╰─────────┬─────────╯
                  ↓
        ┌───────────────────┐
        │                   │
        └─────────┬─────────┘
                  ↓
        ┌───────────────────┐
        │ main sequence star│
        └─────────┬─────────┘
                  ↓
        ┌───────────────────┐
        │                   │
        └─────────┬─────────┘
                  ↓
        ┌───────────────────┐
        │     supernova     │
        └─────────┬─────────┘
                  ↓
        ┌───────────────────┐
        │                   │
        └──────┬─────┬──────┘
   ┌───────────┘     └───────────┐
┌──────────────┐        ┌──────────────┐
│              │        │              │
└──────────────┘        └──────────────┘
```

Complete **Figure 1.1** by writing the names of the **four** missing stages for such a star.

[4 marks]

01.2 Describe what is meant by a **supernova.**

.... **[1 mark]**

02.1 Explain the difference between the terms **speed** and **velocity**.

....

.... **[1 mark]**

02.2 Typical walking speed is 1.5 m/s

Calculate the distance travelled by a person walking at this typical speed for 60 s

Use the following equation.

$$distance = speed \times time$$

....

Distance = ... m **[2 marks]**

02.3 The graph in **Figure 2.1** shows the motion of a cyclist during the first two seconds of a race.

Figure 2.1

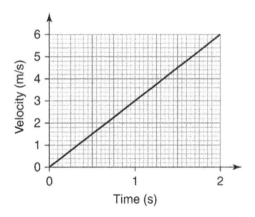

What is the correct description of the motion of the cyclist?

Tick **one** box.

accelerating ☐

decelerating ☐

constant velocity ☐ **[1 mark]**

Question 2 continues on the next page

02.4 The graph in **Figure 2.2** shows the motion of a car on a straight track.

Figure 2.2

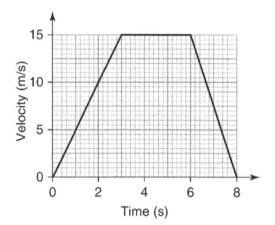

Describe the changing motion of the car shown in **Figure 2.2**

....

....

....

.... **[3 marks]**

03   **Figure 3.1** shows light rays scattered by a surface.

Figure 3.1

03.1   What type of reflection is shown in **Figure 3.1**?

Tick **one** box.

diffuse   ☐

specular   ☐   **[1 mark]**

03.2   How is an object described if light cannot pass through it?

Tick **one** box.

transparent   ☐

translucent   ☐

opaque   ☐   **[1 mark]**

03.3   An object appears red when white light is shone on it.

What colour does the object appear if green light is shone on it?

Tick **one** box.

black   ☐

red   ☐

green   ☐   **[1 mark]**

Question 3 continues on the next page

03.4 White light is made up of a spectrum of different colours.

What has the same value for both red and blue light travelling through a vacuum?

Tick **one** box.

speed ☐

wavelength ☐

frequency ☐

[1 mark]

03.5 An object appears blue when white light shines on it.

What colour does the object appear if it is viewed through a red filter?

Tick **one** box.

blue ☐

red ☐

black ☐

[1 mark]

04.1 A car driver approaches a hazard.

Explain what is meant by the **thinking distance**.

....

.... **[1 mark]**

04.2 Write down **one** factor that can affect thinking distance.

.... **[1 mark]**

04.3 Explain what is meant by the **braking distance**, when someone is driving a car.

....

.... **[1 mark]**

04.4 Write down **one** factor that can affect **braking distance**.

.... **[1 mark]**

04.5 **Figure 4.1** shows changes in thinking distance and braking distance with car speed.

Figure 4.1

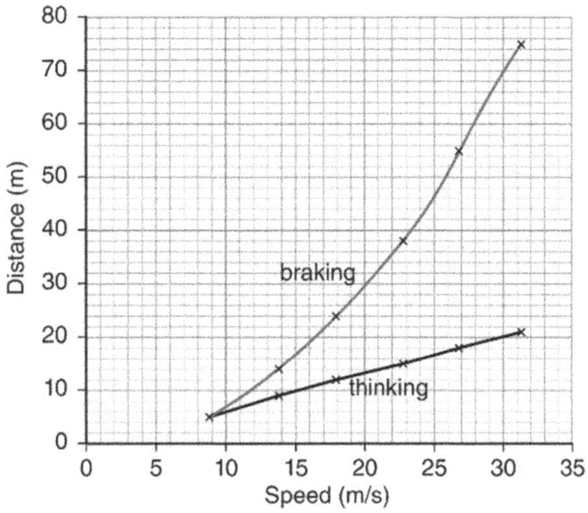

Identify the trend in the **thinking distance** and in the **braking distance**, as the speed of a car varies.

Use the data in the graph in **Figure 4.1**

Thinking distance: ....

....

Braking distance: ....

....

.... **[3 marks]**

Question 4 continues on the next page

04.6 What is the **total stopping distance** for a car travelling at 24 m/s?

Use the data in the graph in **Figure 4.1**

Stopping distance = _____ m **[3 marks]**

04.7 Which energy transfer occurs when the brakes of a moving car are applied?

Tick **one** box.

Chemical energy to kinetic energy ☐

Gravitational potential energy to thermal energy ☐

Kinetic energy to thermal energy ☐ **[1 mark]**

04.8 Write down **one** effect that the energy transfer has on the car's brakes.

_____ **[1 mark]**

05.1 Which of the sentences below correctly describes the effect called **red-shift**?

Tick **one** box.

Red-shift is the observed increase in **speed** of the light from distant galaxies ☐

Red-shift is the observed increase in **wavelength** of the light from distant galaxies ☐

Red-shift is the observed increase in **brightness** of the light from distant galaxies ☐

[1 mark]

05.2 **Figure 5.1** is a sketch graph showing how the recession speed of galaxies varies with their distance measured from Earth.

Figure 5.1

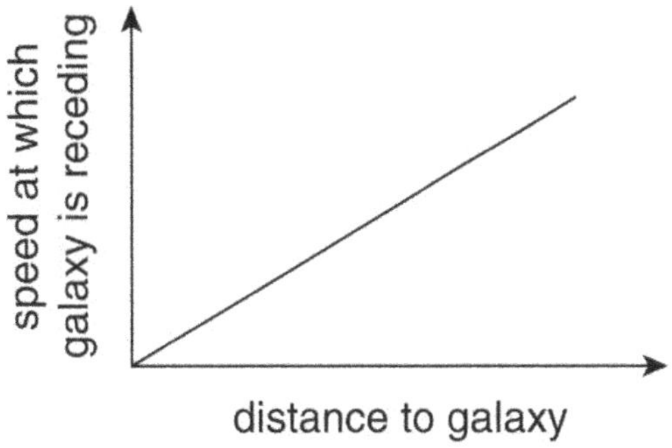

Draw a conclusion from this graph.

....

....

.... [2 marks]

05.3 The data used to produce the graph in **Figure 5.1** provides evidence to support the **Big Bang** theory.

How does the Big Bang theory describe the beginning of the universe?

Tick **one** box.

Cool and very dense ☐

Hot and very dense ☐

Hot with a very low density ☐

[1 mark]

Turn over >

06.1 **Figure 6.1** shows the orbits around the Sun of the four innermost planets of the Solar System.

Figure 6.1

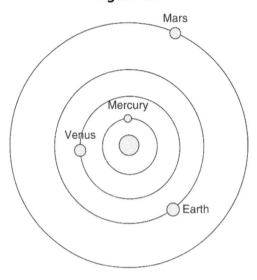

Name the force that keeps the planets in orbit around the Sun.

.... **[1 mark]**

06.2 **Table 6.1** shows the distance of the inner planets from the Sun, and their orbital speed.

Table 6.1

Planet	Distance from Sun in millions of km	Orbital speed in km/s
Mercury	57.9	47.4
Venus	108.2	35.0
Earth	149.6	29.8
Mars	227.9	24.1

Write a conclusion using this data.

....

.... **[1 mark]**

06.3 Jupiter is the **fifth** planet from the Sun. It orbits at a distance of 778.3 million km from the Sun.

Using the data in **Table 6.1**, estimate the orbital speed of Jupiter.

Tick **one** box.

13 km/s ☐

24 km/s ☐

30 km/s ☐ [1 mark]

06.4 **Table 6.2** shows the distance from Jupiter of three of its moons.

Table 6.2

Moon of Jupiter	Distance from Jupiter in millions of km
Europa	0.671
Ganymede	1.07
Callisto	1.883

Which moon will have the greatest orbital speed?

Tick **one** box.

Europa ☐

Ganymede ☐

Callisto ☐ [1 mark]

Turn over >

07   The book on the bench in **Figure 7.1** has a mass of 500 g

Figure 7.1

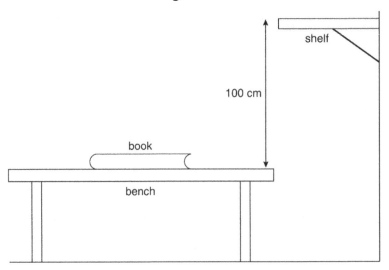

07.1 Write down the equation that links weight, mass and gravitational field strength.

.... **[1 mark]**

07.2 Calculate the weight of the book.

Gravitational field strength = 9.8 N/kg

....

Weight = ... N   **[2 marks]**

07.3 The weight of the book is the force of gravity exerted on the book by the Earth.

Complete the following sentences.

Choose from the words in the box below.

First	Second	Third	mass
Earth	contact	non-contact	weight

According to Newton's _____ Law, the bench exerts a force on

the book equal in size to the book's _____ .

The force of gravity is a type of _____ force.   **[3 marks]**

07.4 A person lifts the book from the bench (**Figure 7.1**).

She lifts it up a distance of 100 cm to put it on the shelf.

Write down the equation which links work done to force and distance moved.

_____ **[1 mark]**

07.5 Calculate the work done by the person in lifting the book onto the shelf.

Give your answer in Nm.

_____

_____

Work done = _____ Nm **[2 marks]**

07.6 Which energy store has increased once the book has been put on the shelf?

Tick **one** box.

Kinetic energy store ☐

Gravitational potential energy store ☐

Elastic potential energy store ☐   **[1 mark]**

Turn over >

08   **Figure 8.1** shows an electromagnet made by a student.

The iron core is clamped vertically.

Figure 8.1

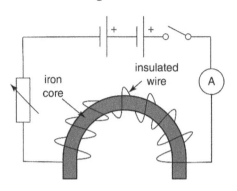

08.1 The student also has an iron nail.

Describe how the student can use this to show that the electromagnet's iron core is only magnetised when there is a current in the wire.

....

....

....

.... **[2 marks]**

08.2 The student wants to measure the strength of her electromagnet.

She uses an iron bar and known masses on a mass hanger, as shown in **Figure 8.2**

Figure 8.2

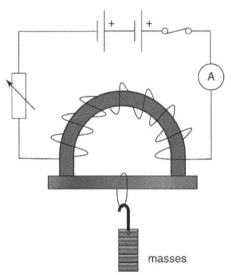

The iron bar is attracted to the electromagnet.

The student gradually adds masses to the hanger.

When the total weight is large enough to overcome the strength of the electromagnet, the iron bar and the hanger with its masses falls to the ground.

The student records the size of the fallen weights:

Weight of iron bar = 1.0 N

Weight of hanger and attached masses = 1.2 N

What is the total weight needed to overcome the strength of the electromagnet?

Total weight = _____ N   **[1 mark]**

08.3 The student wants to investigate how the size of the current in the wire affects the strength of the electromagnet.

Write a step-by-step set of instructions for the student to follow to obtain the data required, using the apparatus in **Figure 8.2**

_____

_____

_____

_____

_____

_____

_____

[4 marks]

08.4 The student records the measurements shown in **Table 8.1**

Table 8.1

Current in A	Total weight supported by electromagnet in N Measurement 1	Total weight supported by electromagnet in N Measurement 2	Total weight supported by electromagnet in N Average
0.5	1.0	1.0	1.0
1.0	2.2	2.0	2.1
1.5	3.0	3.2	3.1
2.0	4.2	4.2	
2.5	5.1	5.3	

Suggest why the student repeated the **total weight** measurements.

_____

_____

[1 mark]

Question 8 continues on the next page

08.5 Complete the **mean total weight** column of **Table 8.1**   **[1 mark]**

08.6 **Figure 8.3** is a graph to show how the maximum total weight supported by the electromagnet depends on the current in the coil.

Figure 8.3

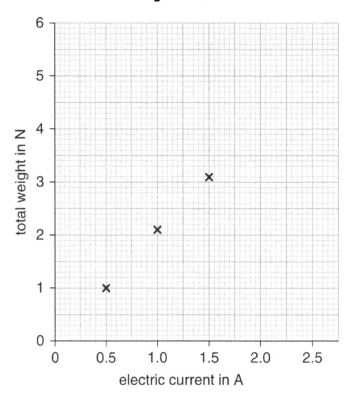

Three data points have been plotted but the graph is incomplete.

Plot the remaining points on **Figure 8.3**, using your completed **Table 8.1**

Draw a line of best fit.   **[2 marks]**

08.7 Write a conclusion about how the size of the electric current in the wire affects the strength of the electromagnet.

Assume that the total weight attached, when the iron bar and weights fall, represents the strength of the electromagnet.

Use your completed graph in **Figure 8.3** to help you write your conclusion.

_____

_____

_____   **[2 marks]**

09 Figure 9.1 shows the groups of waves in the electromagnetic spectrum.

Figure 9.1

Radio waves	Microwaves	Infrared	Visible light	Ultraviolet	X-rays	Gamma waves

09.1 Which group of waves in the electromagnetic spectrum has the **shortest wavelength**?

.... **[1 mark]**

09.2 Which group of waves in the electromagnetic spectrum **causes a sun tan**?

.... **[1 mark]**

09.3 Which group of waves in the electromagnetic spectrum **originates in the nucleus of atoms**?

.... **[1 mark]**

09.4 Which group of waves in the electromagnetic spectrum is emitted by **all** objects?

.... **[1 mark]**

09.5 Write down the equation linking wave speed, frequency and wavelength.

.... **[1 mark]**

Question 9 continues on the next page

09.6 The X-rays used for medical purposes have a wavelength of 2.0×10^{-10} m

They travel at a speed of 3.0×10^8 m/s

Calculate the frequency of the X-rays.

Give a suitable unit with your answer.

Frequency = ...

Unit: .... **[4 marks]**

09.7 **Table 9.1** shows information about doses and risks of some X-ray procedures.

Table 9.1

X-ray procedure	Typical dose in mSv	Equivalent period of background radiation	Lifetime additional risk of fatal cancer
teeth	0.01	1.5 days	1 in a 2 million
chest	0.02	3 days	1 in a million
skull	0.07	11 days	1 in 300 000
neck	0.08	2 weeks	1 in 200 000

[Data from Public Health England]

Suggest **two** conclusions that can be made from the data in **Table 9.1**

1. ....

....

2. ....

.... **[2 marks]**

10.1 Write down the equation that links acceleration, change in velocity, and time.

.... **[1 mark]**

10.2 When a coin is dropped from a tower, it falls freely.

It is not affected by air resistance.

It reaches the ground after falling for 2.0 s

Calculate the velocity of the coin as it reaches the ground.

Take acceleration due to gravity = 10 m/s^2

....

....

Velocity = ... m/s **[3 marks]**

10.3 When a skydiver first jumps out of an aircraft, he accelerates freely downwards.

As his velocity increases, the effect of air resistance gets bigger.

The force of gravity on the skydiver is 600 N

At one instant, the air resistance acting on him is 360 N

What is the resultant force on the skydiver?

Resultant force = ... N **[1 mark]**

10.4 Write down the equation that links resultant force, mass and acceleration.

[1 mark]

....

10.5 The mass of the skydiver is 60 kg

Calculate the skydiver's acceleration at the instant when the air resistance is 360 N

....

....

Acceleration = ... m/s^2 **[3 marks]**

Question 10 continues on the next page

10.6 When the skydiver has been falling for about 20 s, the air resistance acting on him has reached 600 N

What is the resultant force on the skydiver now?

Resultant force = _____ N   **[1 mark]**

10.7 When the skydiver opens his parachute, the air resistance force increases considerably.

Figure 10.1 shows how the skydiver's speed changes, from the time he jumps out of the aircraft to the time he reaches the ground.

Figure 10.1

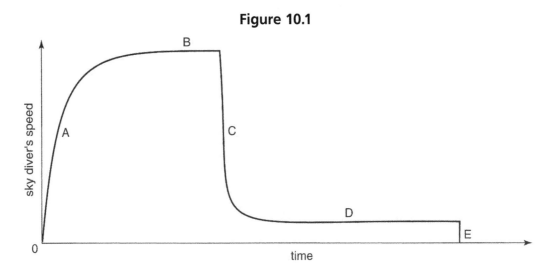

Which section of the graph represents the skydiver travelling at a terminal velocity before his parachute opens?

Tick **one** box.

A	B	C	D	E

[1 mark]

10.8 Which section of the graph represents the skydiver travelling at a terminal velocity after his parachute opens?

Tick **one** box.

A	B	C	D	E

[1 mark]

11.1 The law of reflection of light at a boundary is:

The angle of incidence is equal to the angle of reflection.

A student is asked to demonstrate the law of reflection. Describe a method for this practical demonstration.

Include ways of making the measurements as accurate as possible.

_____

_____

_____

_____

_____

_____

_____

_____

_____

_____

_____

_____

_____

_____

_____

_____ **[6 marks]**

Turn over >

12   A student is to investigate how the size of the resultant force on an object affects the object's acceleration.

He uses the air track and glider shown in **Figure 12.1**

The glider has constant mass.

Figure 12.1

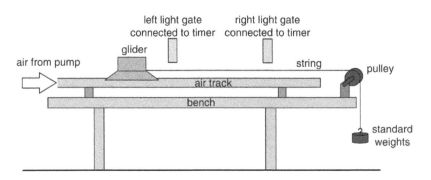

12.1 Identify the independent, dependent variables and control variables.

Independent variable: ....

Dependent variable: ....

Control variable: ....   [3 marks]

12.2 What creates the force that accelerates the glider?

.... [1 mark]

12.3 Air is pumped into the air track, lifting the glider up from the track slightly.

What effect would you expect this to have on the motion of the glider?

Explain your answer.

....

....

.... **[2 marks]**

12.4 The student uses the times recorded by the light gate sensors to calculate the velocity of the glider as it passes through each gate.

One set of the student's measurements is shown in **Table 12.1**

Table 12.1

Velocity through left gate (initial velocity)	0.10 m/s
Velocity through right gate (final velocity)	0.20 m/s
Distance between gates	0.50 m
Force accelerating the glider	0.015 N

Use the following equation to calculate the glider's acceleration.

$(\text{final velocity})^2 - (\text{initial velocity})^2 = 2 \times \text{acceleration} \times \text{distance}$

....

Acceleration = ... m/s^2 **[3 marks]**

12.5 Suggest what the student should do next, to find out how changing the force affects the glider's acceleration.

....

....

.... **[2 marks]**

END OF QUESTIONS

Physics Equation Sheet

Equation Number	Word Equation	Symbol Equation
1	(final velocity)^2 – (initial velocity)^2 = 2 × acceleration × distance	$v^2 - u^2 = 2\,a\,s$
2	elastic potential energy = 0.5 × spring constant × (extension)^2	$E_e = \dfrac{1}{2}\,ke^2$
3	change in thermal energy = mass × specific heat capacity × temperature change	$\Delta E = m\,c\,\Delta\theta$
4	period = $\dfrac{1}{\text{frequency}}$	
5	magnification = $\dfrac{\text{image height}}{\text{object height}}$	
6	thermal energy for a change of state = mass × specific latent heat	$E = m\,L$
7	potential difference across primary coil × current in primary coil = potential difference across secondary coil × current in secondary coil	$V_p I_p = V_s I_s$
8	For gases: pressure × volume = constant	$pV = \text{constant}$

Answers

Question	Answer(s)	Extra info	Mark(s)	AO/Spec ref.
01.1	electrons are transferred from the ruler to the cloth		1	AO1 4.2.5.1
	a deficit/lack of negative electrons on the ruler makes it positively charged		1	
01.2	the cloth becomes negatively charged		1	AO1 4.2.5.1
01.3	at least 4 radial lines drawn from the ball		1	AO1 4.2.5.2
	all arrows drawn on the radial lines are directed outwards		1	
01.4	the particle of dust would move towards the ball		1	AO1 4.2.5.1
	attractive force between ball and dust particle		1	
02.1	two of: particles become (slightly) further apart	any two for 1 mark each	2	AO1 4.3.1.1
	arrangement of particles becomes less ordered			
	particles can move around passing each other			
	speed of vibration / kinetic energy of particles increases as solid heats up, until melting point			
	speed / kinetic energy of particles remains same while oil is changing state from solid to liquid (at melting point)			
02.2	$E = 0.40 \times 250000$	1 mark for substitution	2	AO2 4.3.2.3
	thermal energy = 100 000	1 mark for answer		
	unit: J (or joule)	correct answer with no working shown = 2 marks	1	AO1 4.3.2.3
		1 mark for unit		
02.3	24 (°C)		1	AO3 4.3.2.3
02.4	time taken = 230 – 30		1	AO3 4.3.2.3
	time taken = 200 (s)			

Question	Answer(s)	Extra info	Mark(s)	AO/Spec ref.
03.1	Level 2: A coherent plan covering all major steps presented in a logical order detailing the apparatus used. The plan could be followed by another person to obtain valid results.	3–4	4	AO2 4.3.1.1
	Level 1: Some relevant statements but the plan could not be followed by another person to obtain valid results.	1–2		
	No relevant content	0		
	Indicative content: • mass of block measured • (electronic) balance used to measure mass • length, width and height of block measured • dimensions measured using a rule (or Vernier callipers if the block will fit inside the callipers) • volume calculated from $L \times W \times H$ • substitute the mass and volume data into the density equation			
03.2	A: steel		1	AO3 4.3.1.1
	B: zinc		1	
	C: nickel		1	
04.1	element with a nucleus that has same number of protons		1	AO1 4.4.1.2
	but different number of neutrons		1	
04.2	protons: 53		1	AO1 4.4.1.2
	neutrons 74		1	
	electrons 53		1	
04.3	(nucleus is unstable) and emits radiation		1	AO1 4.4.2.1
	to become more stable		1	
04.4	(high speed) electron is ejected from the nucleus		1	AO1 4.4.2.1
	as a neutron turns into a proton		1	
04.5	time for count-rate to fall by half for one pair of values, e.g. from 200→100: 8 days	maximum 2 marks for determining half-life from only one section of graph	1	AO3 4.4.2.3
	time for count-rate to fall by half for another pair of values, e.g. from 100→50: 8 days	allow 1 mark for correct answer with no working shown	1	
	average = 8 days		1	

Question	Answer(s)	Extra info	Mark(s)	AO/Spec ref.
05.1	they generate heat / they contain a heating element		1	AO1 4.2.4.2
05.2	energy (transferred) = power × time (Accept power = energy transferred / time)		1	AO1 4.2.4.2
05.3	5 hours = 5 × 60 × 60 = 18000 s energy transferred = 50 × 18000 energy transferred = 900000 (J)	1 mark for correct conversion of hours to seconds 1 mark for substitution 1 mark for answer correct answer with no working shown = 3 marks	3	AO2 4.2.4.2
05.4	900000 × 7 = 6 300 000 (J)	allow error carried forward from 05.2	1	AO2 4.2.4.2
06.1	A stretched spring — Elastic potential energy / Thermal energy / Chemical energy; A football that has just been kicked — Kinetic energy	1 mark for each correct line No more than 2 lines	2	AO1 4.1.1.1
06.2	kinetic energy = store of kinetic energy = 0.5 × 50 × 6^2 = 900 J	1 mark for substitution 1 mark for answer correct answer with no working shown = 2 marks	1 1	AO2 4.1.1.2
06.3	gravitational potential energy = mass × gravitational field strength × height		1	AO1 4.1.1.2
06.4	gravitational potential energy = 50 × 9.8 × 10 increase in gravitational potential energy store = 4900 (J)	1 mark for substitution 1 mark for answer correct answer with no working shown = 2 marks	1 1	AO2 4.1.1.2
06.5	kinetic energy = store of kinetic energy = 0.5 × mass × (speed)^2 kinetic energy = 0.5 × 50 × 8^2 store of kinetic energy = 1600 (J)	1 mark for substitution 1 mark for answer correct answer with no working shown = 2 marks	1 1	AO2 4.1.1.2
06.6	energy dissipated = 4900 – 1600 energy dissipated = 3300 (J)	allow error carried forward from 06.4 or 06.5	1	AO2 4.1.2.1

Question	Answer(s)	Extra info	Mark(s)	AO/Spec ref.
07.1	($\Delta E = mc\Delta\theta$) $\Delta E = 0.10 \times 4200 \times 10$ increase in thermal energy of water = 4200 (J)	1 mark for substitution into correct equation 1 mark for answer correct answer with no working shown = 2 marks	1 1	AO2 4.1.1.3
07.2	$\Delta E = 0.10 \times 500 \times 70$ decrease in thermal energy of block = 3500 (J)	1 mark for substitution 1 mark for answer correct answer with no working shown = 2 marks	1 1	AO2 4.1.1.3
07.3	either: Some (thermal) energy is transferred to the beaker. or: Some (thermal) energy is transferred to the surroundings.	Either statement for 1 mark	1	AO1 4.1.2.1
08.1	independent: length dependent: resistance control: thickness		1 1 1	AO3 4.2.1.3
08.2	Level 2: A detailed and coherent plan covering all the major steps is provided. The steps are presented in a logical order that could be followed by another person to obtain valid results.	3–4	4	AO2 4.2.1.3
	Level 1: Simple statements relating to relevant apparatus or steps are made but may not follow a logical sequence. The plan would not enable another person to obtain valid results.	1–2		
	No relevant content	0		

Question	Answer(s)	Extra info	Mark(s)	AO/Spec ref.
	Indicative content • the length of wire between the crocodile clips is measured with a metre rule • the switch is closed • the reading on the ammeter is recorded • the reading on the voltmeter is recorded • the voltmeter reading is divided by the ammeter reading to determine the wire's resistance • switch opened to stop wire overheating • the measurements are repeated for different lengths of wire • plot a graph of resistance against length			
08.3	random error	no other box ticked	1	AO3 4.2.1.3
08.4	straight line, positive gradient, through the origin		1	AO2 4.2.1.3
08.5	length = $\frac{1}{11}$ × 2.2 length = 0.2 (m)	1 mark for correct method of calculation 1 mark for answer correct answer with no working shown = 2 marks	2	AO2 4.2.1.3
09.1	small, well separated circles drawn randomly in the box		1	AO1 4.3.1.1
09.2	moving around randomly / in all directions		1 1	AO1 4.3.3.1
09.3	internal energy		1	AO1 4.3.2.1
09.4	increasing the temperature increases the speed of the gas particles increasing the temperature increases the gas pressure	no more than two boxes ticked	1 1	AO1 4.3.3.1 4.3.2.1
09.5	200 000 × 2000 = p × 2500 p = $\frac{(200\,000 \times 2000)}{2500}$ new pressure = 160 000 (Pa)	1 mark for substitution into correct equation 1 mark for rearranging 1 mark for answer correct answer with no working shown = 3 marks	1 1 1	AO2 4.3.3.2

Question	Answer(s)	Extra info	Mark(s)	AO/Spec ref.
10.1	The potential difference across each resistor has the same value. The resistors are connected in series.	no more than two boxes ticked	2	AO1 4.2.2
10.2	total resistance = 5.0 + 5.0 + 5.0 total resistance = 15.0 (Ω)		1	AO2 4.2.2
10.3	potential difference = current × resistance	allow $V = IR$	1	AO1 4.2.1.3
10.4	1.5 = I × 15 $I = \frac{1.5}{15}$ current = 0.10 (A) (accept 0.1)	1 mark for substitution 1 mark for rearranging 1 mark for answer correct answer with no working shown = 3 marks	1 1 1	AO2 4.2.1.3
10.5	charge = current × time	allow $Q = I\,t$	1	AO1 4.2.1.2
10.6	time = 5 × 60 = 300 s charge = 0.10 × 300 charge = 30 (C)	1 mark for conversion of minutes to seconds 1 mark for substitution 1 mark for answer	1 1 1	AO2 4.2.1.2
10.7	current directly proportional to pd (or voltage) or resistance is constant as current changes or labelled sketch or description of current against potential difference as straight line graph through origin		1	AO1 4.2.1.4
10.8			1	AO1 4.2.1.1
10.9	any two from: • allows current to flow in only one direction • the current in the reverse direction is zero • the resistance is very large in one direction and not in the other / much larger in one direction than the other		2	AO3 4.2.1.4
11.1	**Wood** is an example of a biofuel. Either **natural gas, coal** or **oil** is an example of a fossil fuel.		1 1	AO1 4.1.3

Question	Answer(s)	Extra info	Mark(s)	AO/Spec ref.

11.2	either:
	
	efficiency =
	<u>useful output energy transfer</u>
	  total input energy transfer
	Or:
	
	efficiency =
	<u>useful power output</u>
	  total power input
			1	**AO1**
				4.1.2.2

11.3	efficiency = $\frac{720}{1200}$ × 100 = 60% or efficiency = $\frac{720}{1200}$ = 0.6	1 mark for substitution 1 mark for answer Allow final answer as % or decimal correct answer with no working shown = 2 marks	2	**AO2** 4.1.2.2
11.4	**Level 3:** Coherent and detailed account with several comparisons of reliability and environmental effects and including both advantages and disadvantages.	5–6	6	**AO3** 4.1.3
	Level 2: Clear account with some valid comparisons of reliability and environmental effect.	3–4		
	Level 1: Some relevant comments regarding reliability and environmental effects but comparisons may not be made. The descriptions are vague and lack sufficient detail.	1–2		
	No relevant content	0		

Question	Answer(s)	Extra info	Mark(s)	AO/Spec ref.
	Indicative content: **Advantages of wind power:** • renewable • does not cause (atmospheric) pollution • no greenhouse gas emissions • does not contribute to climate change • usually windy somewhere in the UK **Disadvantages of wind power:** • unpredictable • not reliable (depends on weather) • possible noise disturbance • possible hazard to birds • may be considered to have a negative visual impact **Advantages of coal power:** • reliable (always available, able to generate continuously) • not dependent on the weather • significant coal reserves worldwide **Disadvantages of coal power:** • not renewable • creates atmospheric pollution (soot, sulfur dioxide) which may cause health problems / harm living things in environment / cause acid rain • produces greenhouse gas emissions • which contribute to climate change / global warming • environmental pollution, loss of habitat in areas where coal is mined • mining can be dangerous			

Set A – Paper 2

Question	Answer(s)	Extra info	Mark(s)	AO/Spec ref.
01.1	(force of) gravity / gravitational attraction		1	**AO1** 4.8.1.1
01.2	cloud of gas and dust → protostar → main sequence star → red giant → white dwarf → black dwarf	1 mark for each correct name in the correct box If a box is left empty or an incorrect answer is given in a box, marks can still be given to other answers that are correct provided they are in the correct sequence.	3	**AO1** 4.8.1.2
01.3	A smaller		1	**AO3**
	B greater		1	4.8.1.2
02.1	5.0 Hz	only one box ticked	1	**AO2** 4.6.1.2
02.2	wavelength	only one box ticked	1	**AO1** 4.6.1.2

Question	Answer(s)	Extra info	Mark(s)	AO/Spec ref.
02.3	speed = 3.0 × 4.0 speed = 12 (cm/s)	1 mark for substitution 1 mark for answer correct answer with no working shown = 2 marks	1 1	AO2 4.6.1.2
02.4	independent variable: depth dependent variable: speed		1 1	AO3 4.6.1.2
02.5	The wave travels faster in deeper water. Wave speed is not directly proportional to depth of water.	Only two boxes ticked	1 1	AO3 4.6.1.2
03.1	force displacement	only two boxes ticked	1 1	AO1 4.5.1.1 4.5.6.1.1
03.2	three of: at first the car speeds up / accelerates in the middle of the journey, the car moves with a steady speed near the end of the journey the car slows down / decelerates the car stops at the end of the journey	1 mark for each correct statement, maximum 3 marks	3	AO3 4.5.6.1.4
03.3	60 (m)		1	AO2 4.5.6.1.4
03.4	average speed $= \frac{60}{4}$ average speed =15 m/s	1 mark for substitution 1 mark for answer correct answer with no working shown = 2 marks	2	AO2 4.5.6.1.2 4.5.6.1.4
04.1	The north pole of a magnet exerts **an attractive force** on the south pole of another magnet. The north pole of a magnet exerts **an attractive force** on a piece of magnetic material such as iron The north pole of a magnet exerts **a repulsive force** on the north pole of another magnet. The south pole of one magnet exerts **a repulsive force** on the south pole of another magnet.		1 1 1 1	AO1 4.7.1.1
04.2	a non-contact force	only one box ticked	1	AO1 4.7.1.1

Question	Answer(s)	Extra info	Mark(s)	AO/Spec ref.
04.3	An induced magnet becomes a magnet only when it is placed in a magnetic field (e.g. of a permanent magnet) and loses its magnetism when removed from the magnetic field. A permanent magnet retains its magnetism		1 1	AO1 4.7.1.1
04.4		1 mark for one arrow on each line pointing from N to S maximum 2 marks	2	AO1 4.7.1.2
04.5	**Level 2:** A clear, detailed plan covering all steps presented in a logical order. The plan could be followed by another person to complete the task as required.	3–4	4	AO2 4.7.1.2
	Level 1: Some relevant statements but the plan could not be followed by another person to complete the task.	1–2		
	No relevant content	0		
	Indicative content: • place the bar magnet on a piece of paper and draw around the magnet • place the compass close to (one end of) the magnet • use a pencil to mark a dot at the point that the needle (of the compass) is pointing • move the compass so that its centre is over the dot just made • put another dot at the point that the needle (of the compass) is now pointing • remove the compass and join the dots with an arrow from the first dot to the 2nd dot • continue in the same way until a complete line is drawn from one point on the magnet to another			
05.1	The resultant force on a stationary object is zero. The resultant force on an object moving with constant velocity is zero.	only two boxes ticked	1 1	AO1 4.5.6.2.1

Question	Answer(s)	Extra info	Mark(s)	AO/Spec ref.
05.2	E	only one box ticked	1	AO1 4.5.6.2.1
05.3	F G	1 mark for each correct letter No more than two boxes ticked	2	AO1 4.5.6.2.1
05.4	Acceleration $\frac{14-10}{2.5}$ Acceleration = 1.6	1 mark for substitution 1 mark for answer correct numerical answer with no working shown = 2 marks	2	AO2 4.5.6.1.5
				AO1 4.5.6.1.5
	Unit: m/s²	1 mark	1	
05.5	resultant force = mass × acceleration	accept $F = ma$	1	AO1 4.5.6.2.2
05.6	resultant force = 4000 × 1.6 resultant force = 6400 (N)	1 mark for substitution 1 mark for answer correct answer with no working shown = 2 marks	2	AO2 4.5.6.2.2
05.7	resistive force = 8000 − 6400 resistive force = 1600 (N)	1 mark for substitution 1 mark for answer correct answer with no working shown = 2 marks	2	AO2 4.5.1.4
06.1	air molecules collide with the surface		1	AO1 4.5.5.2
06.2	pressure = normal force ÷ (surface) area	accept $p = \frac{F}{A}$	1	AO1 4.5.5.1.1
06.3	$100\,000 = \frac{force}{1.8}$ force = 100 000 × 1.8 force = 180000 (N)	1 mark for substitution 1 mark for rearranging 1 mark for answer correct answer with no working shown = 3 marks	3	AO2 4.5.5.1.1
06.4	as height (above sea level) increases, atmospheric pressure decreases		1	AO3 4.5.5.2
06.5	pressure and height data correctly selected for two different heights, one double the other conclusion that the student's suggestion is incorrect		2 1	AO3 4.5.5.2

Question	Answer(s)	Extra info	Mark(s)	AO/Spec ref.
06.6	at sea level there is more air above the person either: the greater weight of air above the person exerts more force or: there are more molecules colliding with a person's surface at sea level		1 1	AO1 4.5.5.2
07.1		1 mark for each of the three correct rays 1 mark for correct position of F	3 1	AO1 4.6.2.5
07.2	distance from the centre of a lens to its principal focus		1	AO1 4.6.2.5
07.3		1 mark each for each complete ray drawn as shown. 1 mark for correct image labelled I	2 1	AO1 4.6.2.5
07.4	measure the height / diameter of the object (actual cross-wire) using a rule / ruler / digital callipers measure the height/diameter of the image of the cross-wire divide the image height/diameter by the object height / diameter		1 1 1 1	AO2 4.6.2.5
07.5	3.0 (accept 3)		1	AO2 4.6.2.5
07.6	the greater the focal length, the greater the magnification (for a constant object distance)		1	AO3 4.6.2.5
07.7	get data for a greater number of lenses use lenses with a greater range of focal lengths plot data on a graph / chart of magnification versus focal length	any two of the first three for 1 mark each additional 1 mark if graph axes specified	3	AO3 4.6.2.5
08.1	the distance from the hinge / pivot to the handle is greater for handle position A than for position B for a bigger distance, the moment / turning effect is greater		1 1	AO1 4.5.4
08.2	moment = force × distance	Accept $M = Fd$	1	AO1 4.5.4
08.3	convert cm to m moment = 2.0 × 0.75 moment = 1.5 (N m)	1 mark for unit conversion 1 mark for substitution 1 mark for answer correct answer with no working shown = 3 marks	3	AO2 4.5.4

Question	Answer(s)	Extra info	Mark(s)	AO/Spec ref.
08.4	an anticlockwise moment		1	AO1 4.5.4
08.5	moment = 200 × 0.4 moment = 80 (N m)	1 mark for substitution 1 mark for answer correct answer with no working shown = 2 marks	2	AO2 4.5.4
08.6	clockwise		1	AO1 4.5.4
08.7	80 (N m)		1	AO2 4.5.4
08.8	force × (1.30 + 0.40) = 80 force = 47 (N)	1 mark for substitution into correct equation 1 mark for answer correct answer with no working showbn = 2 marks 1 mark for answer given to 2 s.f.	3	AO2 4.5.4
09.1	**Level 3:** A coherent plan covering all steps presented in a logical order. The plan could be followed by another person to obtain valid results. Procedures ensure accurate data is obtained.	5–6	6	AO2 4.5.3
	Level 2: A clear plan covering the major steps presented in a logical order. The plan could be followed by another person to obtain valid results.	3–4		
	Level 1: Some relevant statements but the plan could not be followed by another person to obtain valid results.	1–2		
	No relevant content	0		

Question	Answer(s)	Extra info	Mark(s)	AO/Spec ref.

	Indicative content:
	• the length of the unstretched spring is measured using the metre rule
	• a standard / known weight is attached to the spring
	• the length of the spring is indicated by the pointer attached to the bottom of the spring
	• the length of the stretched spring is measured using the metre rule
	• extension is found by subtracting the unstretched length from the stretched length
	• to minimise errors:
	  ∘ view the pointer from the same horizontal level
	  ∘ take repeat readings and average			

09.2	C		1	AO3 4.5.3
09.3	A		1	AO3 4.5.3
09.4	C		1	AO3 4.5.3
09.5	B		1	AO2 4.5.3

Question	Answer(s)	Extra info	Mark(s)	AO/Spec ref.
01.1	alpha	Only one box ticked	1	AO1 4.4.2.1
01.2	gamma	Only one box ticked	1	AO1 4.4.2.1
01.3	beta	Only one box ticked	1	AO1 4.4.2.1
01.4	gamma	Only one box ticked	1	AO1 4.4.2.1
01.5	alpha	Only one box ticked	1	AO1 4.4.2.1
01.6	alpha	Only one box ticked	1	AO1 4.4.2.1
02.1	Two of: Volume (of hot water) (accept reference to using 100 cm³ of water each time) Temperature drop/fall (80°C to 60°C) Use same beaker and lid Room temperature constant	Two correct control variables for 1 mark each	2	AO2 4.1.2.1
02.2	Increasing the number of layers of bubble wrap around the beaker **increases** the time taken for the temperature to drop from 80°C to 60°C.		1	AO3 4.1.2.1
	Increasing the number of layers of bubble wrap around the beaker **decreases** the thermal energy transferred to the surroundings each second		1	
02.3	Additional bar drawn in position 1 with height = 220		1	AO2 4.1.2.1
02.4	Expanded polystyrene		1	AO3 4.1.2.1
03.1	A source of energy that can be replenished/will not run out		1	AO1 4.1.3
03.2	Any one from: wind; solar; tidal; biofuel; wave; hydroelectric power		1	AO1 4.1.3
03.3	National Grid		1	AO1 4.2.4.3
03.4		1 mark for one correct line A maximum of three lines drawn	2	AO1 4.2.3.2
03.5	Earth	Only one box ticked	1	AO1 4.2.3.2

Question	Answer(s)	Extra info	Mark(s)	AO/Spec ref.
03.6	Power = 230 × 3.0 Power = 690	1 mark for substitution into correct equation 1 mark for answer Correct answer with no working shown = 2 marks	2	AO2 4.2.4.1 AO1 4.2.4.1
	Unit: W (accept watt)	1 mark for unit	1	
04.1	1×10^{-10} m	Only one box ticked	1	AO1 4.4.1.1
04.2	Ball of positive charge		1	AO1 4.4.1.3
	Electrons (accept negative charge) embedded throughout the ball		1	
04.3	Positive charge (accept mass) concentrated in small central nucleus		1	AO1 4.4.1.3
	Electrons surround (orbit) the nucleus		1	
04.4	Neutron		1	AO1 4.4.1.3
	Proton		1	
	(in either order)			
05.1		1 mark for each correct line A maximum of 3 lines	3	AO1 4.1.1.1
05.2	Elastic potential energy		1	AO1 4.1.1.2
05.3	energy stored $= \frac{1}{2} \times 25 \times 0.12^2$ energy stored = 0.18 (J)	1 mark for substitution 1 mark for answer Correct answer with no working shown = 2 marks	2	AO2 4.1.1.2
06.1	**Level 2:** A coherent description of the steps required to demonstrate: repulsion between like charges AND attraction between unlike charges. For the maximum mark, the plan should include the initial step involving charging by friction	3–4	4	AO2 4.2.5.1

Question	Answer(s)	Extra info	Mark(s)	AO/Spec ref.
	Level 1: A clear description of steps that demonstrate EITHER: repulsion between like charges, OR attraction between unlike charges For the maximum mark, the plan should include the initial step involving charging by friction	1–2		
	No relevant content	0		
	Indicative content: The rods can be charged by rubbing with a cloth. Rubbing a rod with a cloth transfers electrons (to or from the rod) A charged acetate rod is brought near to the end of a suspended charged acetate rod to show repulsion between like charges. **Or** a charged polythene rod is brought near to the end of a suspended charged polythene rod to show repulsion between like charges. A charged acetate rod is brought near to the end of a suspended charged polythene rod to show attraction between unlike charges. **Or** a charged polythene rod is brought near to the end of a suspended charged acetate rod to show attraction between unlike charges.			
07.1	Radon gas Radioactive rocks in soil and buildings		1 1	AO3 4.4.3.1
07.2	5.3		1	AO3 4.4.3.1
07.3	$^{222}_{86}Rn \rightarrow {}^{218}_{84}Po + {}^{4}_{2}He$	1 mark each for the two missing numbers	2	AO2 4.4.2.2
07.4	$^{218}_{84}Po \rightarrow {}^{218}_{85}At + {}^{0}_{-1}e$	1 mark each for the three missing numbers	3	AO2 4.4.2.2
08.1	At least one of the free neutrons emitted must cause another uranium nucleus to undergo fission		1 1	AO1 4.4.4.1
08.2	Kinetic	Only one box ticked	1	AO1 4.4.4.1

Question	Answer(s)	Extra info	Mark(s)	AO/Spec ref.
08.3	Either: Explosion caused by a nuclear weapon Or: Explosion caused by (nuclear) reactor	Allow 'nuclear bomb'	1	AO1 4.4.4.1
08.4	Caesium-137 Krypton-85		1 1	AO3 4.4.2.4
08.5	They have the longest half-lives so will be radioactive for a long time/many years causing a hazard to health (and living things in the environment) (unless stored safely)		1 1 1	AO3 4.4.2.4
08.6	(nuclear) fusion		1	AO1 4.4.4.2
09.1	The energy needed to raise the temperature of 1 kg of a material by 1°C		1	AO1 4.1.1.3
09.2	Thermometer C Because it covers the required temperature range / B cannot cover range And has best (smallest) resolution in that temperature range / can measure smaller temperature change than A or D		1 1 1	AO3 4.1.1.3
09.3	Temperature rise = 23.0°C (accept 23°C) $21260 = 1.00 \times c \times 23.0$ $c = \frac{21260}{1.00 \times 23.0}$ $c = 924$ (J/kg °C) Answer given to 3 significant figures	1 mark 1 mark for substitution 1 mark for rearranging 1 mark for answer Correct answer with no working shown = 4 marks 1 mark	5	AO2 4.1.1.3
10.1	Thermistor		1	AO1 4.2.1.1
10.2	The resistance decreases/gets smaller as the temperature increases		1	AO3 4.2.1.4
10.3	The total resistance in the circuit decreases (because the resistance of Q decreases). (Since $I = \frac{V}{R}$) the ammeter reading increases.		1 1	AO2 4.2.1.4
10.4	400 (Ω)		1	AO3 4.2.1.4
10.5	Total resistance = 800 + 400 Total resistance = 1200 (Ω)	1 mark	1	AO2 4.2.2

Question	Answer(s)	Extra info	Mark(s)	AO/Spec ref.
10.6	Potential difference = current × resistance	Accept $V = I R$	1	AO1 4.2.1.3
10.7	$6.0 = I \times 1200$ $I = \frac{6.0}{1200}$ $I = 0.0050$ (A) (accept 0.005)	1 mark for substitution 1 mark for rearranging 1 mark for answer Allow error carried forward from 10.5 Correct answer with no working shown = 3 marks	3	AO2 4.2.1.3
10.8	Power = (current)^2 × resistance	Accept $P = I^2R$	1	AO1 4.2.4.1
10.9	Power = 0.0050^2 × 800 Power = 0.02 (W) Power = 20 (mW)	1 mark for substitution 1 mark for answer Allow error carried forward from 10.7 1 mark for answer in mW Correct answer (in mW) with no working shown = 3 marks	3	AO2 4.2.4.1
11.1		1 mark for ammeter in a complete circuit 1 mark for voltmeter in a complete circuit in parallel with X 1 mark for variable resistor in the main circuit	3	AO1 4.2.1.4
11.2	Charge = current × time	Accept $Q = I t$	1	AO1 4.2.1.2
11.3	Charge = 0.12 × 10 Charge = 1.2 (C)	1 mark for substitution 1 mark for answer Correct answer with no working shown = 2 marks	2	AO2 4.2.1.2
11.4	Energy = charge × potential difference	Accept $E = QV$	1	AO1 4.2.4.2

Question	Answer(s)	Extra info	Mark(s)	AO/Spec ref.
11.5	Energy transferred = 1.2 × 0.60 Energy transferred = 0.72 (J)	1 mark for substitution 1 mark for answer Allow error carried forward from 11.3 Correct answer with no working shown = 2 marks	2	AO2 4.2.4.2
11.6	Constant up to 0.7 V/0.14 A and then increases EITHER: at least two calculations using $R = \frac{V}{I}$ to obtain resistance values at different currents OR: reference made to trend in the change in current corresponding to a change in potential difference	1 mark 1 mark 1 mark for justification	3	AO3 4.2.1.3 4.2.1.4
12.1	Molecules in (liquid) water are much closer together than in water vapour in number of particles per unit volume Water vapour is mostly empty space compared with liquid water Liquid water is denser than water vapour in number of particles per unit volume		1 1 1	AO3 4.3.1.1
12.2	**Level 3:** A coherent plan covering all steps presented in a logical order detailing all the apparatus used. The plan could be followed by another person to obtain a valid result for the density of the oil.	5–6	6	AO2 4.3.1.1

Question	Answer(s)	Extra info	Mark(s)	AO/Spec ref.
	Level 2: A clear plan covering most of the major steps presented in a logical order detailing the apparatus used. The plan could be followed by another person to obtain valid results for the mass and volume of the oil.	3–4		
	Level 1: Some relevant statements but the plan could not be followed by another person to obtain valid results.	1–2		
	No relevant content	0		
	Indicative content: Mass of empty measuring cylinder is measured			
	Mass measured with (electronic) balance			
	Oil poured into measuring cylinder			
	Volume of oil in measuring cylinder recorded			
	Mass of measuring cylinder with oil measured (with balance)			
	Mass of oil found by subtracting the mass of the empty measuring cylinder from the mass of the cylinder with oil			
	Density found by dividing the mass of oil by the volume			

Set B – Paper 2

Question	Answer(s)	Extra info	Mark(s)	AO/Spec ref.
01.1	cloud of gas and dust / protostar / main sequence star / red super giant / supernova / neutron star / black hole	1 mark for each correct name in the sequence shown. Neutron star and black hole in either order	4	AO1 4.8.1.2
01.2	The explosion of a massive star		1	AO1 4.8.1.2
02.1	Velocity of an object is its speed in a given/specific direction	Allow 'speed is a scalar, velocity is a vector'	1	AO1 4.5.6.1.3

Question	Answer(s)	Extra info	Mark(s)	AO/Spec ref.
02.2	Distance = 1.5 × 60	1 mark for substitution	1	AO2 4.5.6.1.2
	Distance = 90 (m)	1 mark for answer. Correct answer with no working shown = 2 marks	1	
02.3	accelerating	Only one box ticked	1	AO1 4.5.6.1.5
02.4	Three different stages in the following order: Constant acceleration, constant velocity, constant deceleration/ negative acceleration **Or** acceleration of 5 m/s²; constant velocity of 15 m/s; deceleration of 7.5 m/s²/ acceleration of −7.5 m/s² **Or** time intervals specified for acceleration, constant velocity, deceleration	1 mark each, must be in the order shown	3	AO3 4.5.6.1.5
03.1	diffuse	Only one box ticked	1	AO1 4.6.2.6
03.2	opaque	Only one box ticked	1	AO1 4.6.2.6
03.3	black	Only one box ticked	1	AO1 4.6.2.6
03.4	speed	Only one box ticked	1	AO1 4.6.2.6
03.5	black	Only one box ticked	1	AO1 4.6.2.6
04.1	Distance travelled by the car during the driver's reaction time.		1	AO1 4.5.6.3.1
04.2	One from: Tiredness Drugs Alcohol (A named source of) distraction (such as mobile phone)	Any one for 1 mark	1	AO1 4.5.6.3.2
04.3	Distance travelled by the car while the brakes are being applied		1	AO1 4.5.6.3.1

Question	Answer(s)	Extra info	Mark(s)	AO/Spec ref.
04.4	One from: Wet road Icy road Condition of tyres Condition of brakes Gradient of road Surface of road	Any one for 1 mark	1	AO1 4.5.6.3.3
04.5	Thinking distance: increases steadily with increasing speed Braking distance: increases with increasing speed (Braking distance:) at an increasing rate		1 1 1	AO3 4.5.6.3.1
04.6	Thinking distance = 16 m (accept 15-17) Braking distance = 42 m (accept 41-43) Stopping distance = 58 (m) (accept 56-60)	1 mark 1 mark 1 mark Correct answer with no working 3 marks	3	AO2 4.5.6.3.1
04.7	Kinetic energy to thermal energy	Only one box ticked	1	AO1 4.5.6.3.4
04.8	Temperature of brakes rises Or Brakes become worn	Accept either statement for 1 mark	1	AO1 4.5.6.3.4
05.1	Red-shift is the observed increase in wavelength of the light from distant galaxies	Only one box ticked	1	AO1 4.8.2
05.2	The speed at which a galaxy recedes gets larger as the distance gets larger Speed of galaxy receding is directly proportional to distance	1 mark for a basic conclusion Or 2 marks for a more specific conclusion	2	AO3 4.8.2
05.3	Hot and very dense	Only one box ticked	1	AO1 4.8.2
06.1	gravity		1	AO1 4.8.1.3
06.2	The greater the distance from the Sun, the lower the orbital speed		1	AO3 4.8.1.3
06.3	13 km/s	Only one box ticked	1	AO2 4.8.1.3
06.4	Europa	Only one box ticked	1	AO3 4.8.1.3

Question	Answer(s)	Extra info	Mark(s)	AO/Spec ref.
07.1	Weight = mass × gravitational field strength	Accept $W = mg$	1	AO1 4.5.1.3
07.2	500 g converted to 0.5(00) kg Weight = 0.5(00) × 9.8 = 4.9 (N)	1 mark for unit conversion 1 mark for substitution and answer Correct answer with no working shown = 2 marks	2	AO2 4.5.1.3
07.3	According to Newton's **Third** Law, the bench exerts a force on the book equal in size to the book's **weight**. The force of gravity is a **non-contact** force.	1 mark for each correctly substituted word	3	AO1 4.5.6.2.3 4.5.1.2
07.4	Work done = force × distance moved	Accept $W = F\,d$	1	AO1 4.5.2
07.5	100 cm converted to 1(.00) m Work done = 4.9 × 1(.00) = 4.9 (N m)	1 mark for unit conversion 1 mark for substitution and answer Correct answer with no working shown = 2 marks	2	AO2 4.5.2
07.6	Gravitational potential energy store	Only one box ticked	1	AO1 4.1.1.2
08.1	Demonstrate that nail is attracted to the core/electromagnet when switch closed/current flowing. Observe nail fall/cease to be attracted when switch opened		1 1	AO1 4.7.2.1
08.2	Total weight = 2.2 (N)		1	AO2 4.7.2.1
08.3	**Level 2:** A clear plan covering all steps presented in a logical order. The plan could be followed by another person to obtain valid results	3–4	4	AO2 4.7.2.1
	Level 1: Some relevant statements but the plan could not be followed by another person to obtain valid results.	1–2		
	No relevant content	0		

Question	Answer(s)	Extra info	Mark(s)	AO/Spec ref.
	Indicative content:			
	Close the switch			
	Adjust the variable resistor to set the current to a chosen value			
	Record ammeter reading			
	Choose an ammeter with an appropriate resolution for the range of current readings (use trial runs as necessary)			
	Gradually add masses in small increments to the bar			
	Until the bar falls			
	Care should be taken to avoid injury (e.g. to the feet) when the iron bar and masses fall			
	By placing soft material below the electromagnet			
	Add the weight of the bar to the weight of the masses attached to the bar to get the attractive force exerted by the electromagnet			
	Repeat the procedure and calculate an average total weight for that current			
	Repeat with several different current values			
	To produce several data sets of current and total weight/ attractive force			
08.4	To minimise effect of (random) errors Or To help spot anomalous data Or To check results are repeatable	1 mark for either statement	1	AO3 4.7.2.1
08.5	4.2 5.2	1 mark if both values are correct	1	AO2 4.7.2.1
08.6	Two points correctly plotted Straight line of best fit drawn that passes through the origin	1 mark if both points correctly plotted 1 mark for suitable line of best fit	2	AO2 4.7.2.1
08.7	Increasing the current increases the strength of the electromagnet And either: The strength is directly proportional to the current Or: Doubling the current doubles the strength	1 mark for a basic conclusion Or 2 marks for a detailed conclusion referring to direct proportionality	2	AO3 4.7.2.1

Question	Answer(s)	Extra info	Mark(s)	AO/Spec ref.
09.1	gamma		1	AO1 4.6.2.1
09.2	ultraviolet		1	AO1 4.6.2.4
09.3	gamma		1	AO1 4.6.2.3
09.4	infrared		1	AO1 4.6.3.1
09.5	(Wave) speed = frequency × wavelength	Accept: $v = f\lambda$	1	AO1 4.6.1.2
09.6	$3.0 \times 10^8 =$ frequency $\times 2.0 \times 10^{-10}$ frequency $= \dfrac{3.0 \times 10^8}{2.0 \times 10^{-10}}$ Frequency $= 1.5 \times 10^{18}$ Unit: Hz	1 mark for substitution 1 mark for rearranging 1 mark for answer Correct answer with no working shown = 3 marks 1 mark for unit	3 1	AO2 4.6.1.2 AO1 4.6.1.2
09.7	Two of: X-ray procedures are a risk to health / can cause (fatal) cancer X-ray procedures on different parts of the body present different sized risks Lower doses give lower risk (of fatal cancer) The higher the (X-ray) dose, the longer the equivalent period of background radiation Some X-ray procedures have doses comparable with background radiation levels The risk of any single X-ray procedure is less than the risk of a 2-week period of background radiation	Any two conclusions for 1 mark each Accept any other sensible conclusion consistent with the data	2	AO3 4.6.2.3
10.1	acceleration = $\dfrac{\text{change in velocity}}{\text{time}}$ or Acceleration = (change in velocity) ÷ time	Accept $a = \dfrac{\Delta v}{t}$ Accept $a = (v-u)/t$	1	AO1 4.5.6.1.5

Question	Answer(s)	Extra info	Mark(s)	AO/Spec ref.
10.2	$10 = \dfrac{\text{change in velocity}}{2.0}$ Initial velocity = 0 Final velocity = 10 × 2.0 Velocity = 20 (m/s)	1 mark for substitution 1 mark for indication that initial velocity = 0 and for rearranging 1 mark for answer Correct answer with no working shown = 3 marks	3	AO2 4.5.6.1.5
10.3	Resultant force = 240 (N)		1	AO2 4.5.6.1.5
10.4	Resultant force = mass × acceleration	Accept $F = m\,a$	1	AO1 4.5.6.2.2
10.5	$240 = 60 ×$ acceleration Acceleration = $\dfrac{240}{60}$ Acceleration = 4.0 (m/s²) (accept 4)	1 mark for correct substitution 1 mark for rearranging 1 mark for answer Correct answer with no working shown = 3 marks	3	AO2 4.5.6.2.2
10.6	Resultant force = 0 (N)		1	AO2 4.5.6.1.5
10.7	B	Only one box ticked	1	AO3 4.5.6.1.5
10.8	D	Only one box ticked	1	AO3 4.5.6.1.5
11.1	**Level 3:** A detailed and coherent plan covering all steps presented in a logical order. The plan could be followed by another person to obtain sufficient valid results to confirm the law of reflection. Procedures to ensure and assess accuracy are considered. **Level 2:** A clear plan covering the major steps presented in a logical order. The plan could be followed by another person to obtain valid results.	5–6 3–4	6	AO2 4.6.1.3

Question	Answer(s)	Extra info	Mark(s)	AO/Spec ref.
	Level 1: Some relevant statements but the plan could not be followed by another person to obtain valid results.	1–2		
	No relevant content	0		
	Indicative content: Position a plane mirror vertically on a piece of paper Draw a line on the paper along the front edge of the mirror Remove the mirror, and, using a protractor, draw a line at 90° to the first line (the normal) Use a protractor to draw a line at a specific angle to the normal and label this line 'incident ray' Replace the mirror on the paper along the original line Direct a ray of light from a ray box along the line marked incident ray Mark a series of dots along the middle of the reflected ray Join the dots (with a pencil) to show the path of the reflected ray. Measure the angle of reflection with the protractor Repeat for at least 3 different incident angles Repeat for each chosen angle of incidence to assess the accuracy/repeatability of the measurements			
12.1	Independent variable: (resultant) force		1	AO3 4.5.6.2.2
	Dependent variable: acceleration		1	
	Control variable: mass (of glider) (accept: same glider or same air track set up)		1	
12.2	(Standard) weights (attached to the string)		1	AO1 4.5.6.2.2
12.3	Glider moves freely/more smoothly / accelerates easily		1	AO1 4.5.6.2.2
	Because friction removed/reduced		1	
12.4	$0.20^2 – 0.10^2 = 2$ × acceleration × 0.50 acceleration = $\dfrac{0.20^2 – 0.10^2}{(2 × 0.50)}$ Acceleration = 0.030 (m/s²) (accept 0.03)	1 mark for substitution 1 mark for rearranging 1 mark for answer Correct answer with no working = 3 marks	3	AO2 4.5.6.1.5
12.5	Take measurements for a range of different forces.		1	AO2 4.5.6.2.2
	Plot a graph of acceleration against force.		1	

BLANK PAGE

BLANK PAGE